PROGGY
MENAGERIE

PROGGY
MENAGERIE

HAYLEY SMITH
Founder of Craft Yourself Silly

Skyhorse Publishing books may be purchased in bulk at special discounts for sales promotion, corporate gifts, fund-raising, or educational purposes. Special editions can also be created to specifications. For details, contact the Special Sales Department, Skyhorse Publishing, 307 West 36th Street, 11th Floor, New York, NY 10018 or info@skyhorsepublishing.com.

Skyhorse® and Skyhorse Publishing® are registered trademarks of Skyhorse Publishing, Inc.®, a Delaware corporation.

Visit our website at www.skyhorsepublishing.com.

10 9 8 7 6 5 4 3 2 1

Library of Congress Cataloging-in-Publication Data is available on file.

Project Editor: Julie Brooke
Proofreader: Cassie Armstrong
Designer: Leah Germann
Cover design: Leah Germann
Cover photo: Craft Yourself Silly
Print ISBN: 978-1-68099-337-0
Ebook ISBN: 978-1-68099-338-7

Printed in China

Contents

Introduction

"Proggy" is the colloquial term used in the northeast of England—the area where I was born and live and work today—for a rag rug. But, depending where you travel in the UK, you'll find many names for the same technique: "clippy," "hooky," "proddy," and many, many more.

I discovered the technique while running a pancake café and pottery painting studio with my mother. We saw a big resurgence in interest for learning traditional craft skills, and one of the things we were asked was how to make rag rugs. I taught myself the basics, and once I realized how simple the proggy technique was, I saw it had the potential to be used for more than just the humble rug.

Until the mid-twentieth century, a proggy mat was a staple in the Northumberland home. Traditionally created from old clothes, making the mat was an annual event, recycling and reusing fabrics long before it was fashionable. The newly made mat went onto the bed to keep your toes warm and toasty during cold Northumberland nights. The one that used to be on the bed went onto the bedroom floor, and the old rugs then cascaded down the pecking order, with the oldest ones being used in the kitchen.

The strips for the rug were traditionally cut out using the side of a matchbox as a guide to keep them all the same size, and potato sacks were used for the backing. The fabrics used were old woolen coats in blacks, browns, grays, and blues. Today, these heavy, cumbersome fabrics have been replaced with lighter materials in a rainbow of colors. And it's not just the colors you can experiment with. Modern fabrics such as fleece are lightweight, which means you can make proggy bags and soft toys that are soft and easy to carry, as well as wall hangings, pillows, bags, throws, and even clothes.

My first proggy project was Graham the Hedgehog—how could I not? His spikes were just the perfect partner for the proggy technique. We then launched Proggy® rag rug kits on one of the television shopping channels in the United Kingdom, and were overwhelmed by the positive response that we had for the craft. At that point Craft Yourself Silly was born, and it became a company in its own right, specializing in fabric crafts.

The next additions to our Proggy® family were Alan the Owl and Bill the Badger, inspired by the men who worked in the office next door. From then on, all of the creatures in our kits have been named after friends and family who have been involved in our Proggy® journey. The collection has expanded to include more than thirty soft toys, a Christmas and Halloween range, lots of interior design projects, and a variety of bags.

Proggy® launched in the United States in 2015 to an amazing reception and won regional and national export awards. Proggy® products now appear all over the world, and we're proud to have taken a local, traditional craft and created a fun and friendly product that is available to a global market.

We hope you enjoy the projects in this book as much as we have.

HAYLEY SMITH

Woodland
Creatures

As night falls in the woods, fox, badger, and hedgehog emerge from their burrows to search for food. As the busy part of their day begins, the squirrel's search for nuts and leaves comes to an end and he nestles down to sleep.

Friendly Fox

This little fellow is always making mischief, wagging his bushy orange tail, and poking his pointy nose into everyone's business. You can't help but love him.

You will need

20 x 20 in. (50 x 50cm) burlap

40 x 20 in. (100 x 50cm) orange fleece

40 x 20 in. (100 x 50cm) white fleece

6 x 6 in. (15 x 15cm) black fleece

one pair ½-in. (12mm) black safety eyes

one ½-in. (12mm) black safety nose

10 oz. (250g) polyester soft toy stuffing

orange or white sewing thread

fabric marking pen

scissors

ruler

pointed rag rug tool

sewing needle

fabric glue (optional)

Difficulty rating

Intermediate

Completed size

8 x 5 x 5 in. (20 x 13 x 13cm)

Prepare the pieces

1 Using the templates on page 108, cut out the body and tail sections from burlap and copy the markings. Cut out two ears, the snout, and feet from black, white, and orange fleece as directed on the templates. Cut a strip ½ x 10 in. (1.5 x 25cm) from the orange fleece; this will be used to attach the tail to the body. Cut the remaining orange and white fleece into ½ x 2 in. (1.5 x 5cm) strips (see template on page 101).

Hook the pieces

2 Fold the burlap for the front of the body along the marked lines and use the technique shown on page 102 to secure the fold. Fill the outline of the body using the technique shown on page 102. Continue until the folded edge is secure. Repeat for the back of the body and the tail, adding in the tummy section and the tip of the tail in white. Once the outline is complete, trim any excess burlap using scissors.

Add the eyes and ears

3 Attach the safety eyes in the positions marked on the template using the technique on page 105.

4 To add the ears, push the two strips of fabric at the base of one ear through the burlap on one side of the head as marked on the template, then tie them together using the technique on page 105. Keep the strips three strands of burlap apart. Repeat on the other side of the head.

Adding the snout

5 Stab stitch the orange snout section onto the white snout section, positioning it as shown on the template. Green thread is used in the photograph to show the stitches.

6 Fold the snout in half so the orange section is on the inside and backstitch the straight edges together, leaving a small gap at the tip and the seam allowance shown on the template. Turn the snout right side out and insert the safety nose through the hole in the tip, using the same technique as for the eyes.

7 Fill in the body and tail sections using the technique shown on page 102. Do not fill in the section where the snout will sit.

8 To attach the snout, align the center of the snout with the corresponding section of the burlap. Push four strips of fabric from the snout (one each for the top, bottom, left, and right) through the burlap and adjust until you are happy with the position. Push through the remaining strips and tie together in pairs using double knots. Secure with fabric glue if desired.

Add the tail

9 Fold the strip of orange fleece for the tail in half (shown here in black) and push both ends through the base of one of the tail sections hooked in step 2. Work from the wrong to the right side, and insert them three strands of burlap apart. Hold the tail sections with the wrong sides facing each other and oversew together, adding stuffing as you go.

10 Position the tail on the body and insert the fabric strips through the burlap, three strands apart. Tie the ends together using a double knot. Secure with fabric glue if desired.

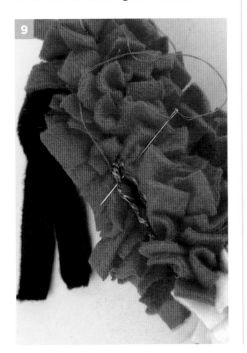

Complete the fox

11 Put the front and back body together with the wrong sides facing each other. Starting at the bottom, sew the two pieces together, leaving a gap large enough to push the stuffing through. Stuff the body, then oversew the opening closed.

12 Position the feet section at the base of the body and push the feet through the burlap using the pointed tool. Oversew the feet to the edge of the burlap sections. If necessary, use scissors to trim the fleece covering the fox body so it is a uniform length.

Try This!

T-shirt texture

Try using T-shirt fabric for this project—the edges of the strips will roll together as you work to create a furry texture.

Big Bold Badger

Foraging for bugs in the dead of night is where you would most often find this inquisitive chap, but his stripy snout loves a good hug too.

You will need

40 x 20 in. (100 x 50cm) burlap

60 x 20 in. (150 x 50cm) gray fleece

10 x 10 in. (25 x 25cm) white fleece

8 x 5 in. (20 x 12cm) black fleece

one pair ½-in. (12mm) black safety eyes

10 oz. (250g) polyester soft toy stuffing

black or white sewing thread

fabric marking pen

scissors

ruler

pointed rag rug tool

sewing needle

fabric glue (optional)

seam ripper (optional)

Difficulty rating

Challenging

Completed size

11½ x 6¾ x 6¼ in. (29 x 17 x 16cm)

Prepare the pieces

1 Using the templates on page 109, cut out two body sections from burlap and copy the markings. Cut out the tummy, snout, stripes, nose, ears, and eyes from black, white, and gray fleece as directed on the templates. Cut a strip ½ x 10 in. (1.5 x 25cm) from the gray fleece; this will be used to secure the edges of the face. Cut the remaining gray fleece into ½ x 2 in. (1.5 x 5cm) strips (see template on page 101).

Hook the pieces

2 To secure the edges of the burlap face section, use the long strip of gray fleece to create a running stitch around the folded edge using the technique shown on page 106.

3 Secure the remaining edges of the burlap body sections with strips of gray fleece using the technique shown on page 103. Fill the outline, then trim any excess burlap using scissors. Fill in the body sections, but not the face, using the technique shown on page 102.

Join the body sections

4 Hold the body sections with the wrong sides together. Oversew from the tail to the neck (marked A–B on the template). Fold the front legs in half lengthwise toward the back of the badger, then oversew to make feet. Leave the front section open.

5 Position the tummy section against the base of the body with the wrong sides facing, tucking the seam allowance shown on the template inside the body. Oversew in place.

Make the face

6 Position the black fleece stripes on the white fleece snout as shown in the photograph. Stab stitch along each edge to hold in place (see page 106).

7 Fold the snout in half, with the wrong sides together, and backstich around the outside edges, leaving the seam allowance shown on the template, to create a pocket. Turn the snout right side out and slip it over the burlap face section to check the fit and adjust as necessary. When you are happy with the fit, position the snout on the body and oversew in position.

Add the ears

8 Position the ears at the top of the snout and about ½ in. (1.5cm) apart. Make one hole in the snout for each ear using the tip of a pair of scissors or a seam ripper. Push the two strips at the base of the ears through the holes in the snout and the burlap and secure using the technique shown on page 105. Secure with fabric glue if desired.

Add the eyes

9 Make a hole in the center of the white fleece circles and position on the snout. Attach the circles to the snout using the safety eyes and the technique shown on page 105.

Completing the badger

10 Position the nose at the tip of the snout and backstitch in place.

11 Stuff the body, then oversew the opening between the front legs closed. If necessary, use scissors to trim the fleece covering the badger body so it is a uniform length, being careful not to cut the ears.

Try This!

A new coat

People traditionally used old gray coats to create proggy rugs. You can use this traditional fabric to give the badger's fur a rougher texture. You can also use the proggy technique for the striped face rather than sewing it on.

Happy Hedgehog

This prickly pal would be welcome in any home instead of snuffling among the fall leaves in search of somewhere soft and warm to sleep through the winter.

You will need

20 x 10 in. (50 x 25cm) burlap

20 x 20 in. (50 x 50cm) brown fleece

8 x 8 in. (20 x 20cm) beige fleece

one pair ½-in. (12mm) black safety eyes

10 oz. (250g) polyester soft toy stuffing

brown and beige sewing thread

fabric marking pen

scissors

ruler

pointed rag rug tool

sewing needle

fabric glue (optional)

Difficulty rating

Easy

Completed size

4 x 4¾ x 7¾ in. (10 x 12 x 17cm)

Prepare the pieces

1 Using the templates on page 110, cut out the body sections and base from burlap and copy the markings. Cut out the face from beige fleece as directed on the template. Cut two strips, ½ x 10 in. (1.5 x 25cm), from the beige fleece; this will be used to secure the edges of the burlap face and base. Cut the remaining brown fleece into ½ x 2 in. (1.5 x 5cm) strips with pointed ends (see template on page 101).

Hook the pieces

2 To secure the edges of the burlap face sections, use the long strips of beige fleece to create a running stitch around the folded edge using the technique shown on page 103.

3 Secure the edges of the burlap body sections with strips of brown fleece using the technique shown on page 103. Once the outline is complete, trim any excess burlap using scissors.

4 Fill in the body sections using the technique shown on page 102.

Join the body sections

5 Hold the body sections with the wrong sides together. Starting at the nose and stitching toward the tail, oversew the sections together. Do not sew the base together. Red thread is used in the photograph to show the stitches.

Make the face

6 Fold the face section in half with the wrong sides together and backstitch along the narrow end (marked A–B on the template), leaving the seam allowance shown on the template. Purple thread is used in the photograph to show the stitches.

7 Turn the face section right side out and use your fingers to smooth the seam flat.

8 Position the face over the burlap head section and oversew in place using small stitches.

9 Using the template markings as a guide, cut a small hole for one of the eyes in the face (do not cut the burlap beneath it). Attach one of the safety eyes using the technique shown on page 105. Repeat on the other side.

Completing the hedgehog

10 Position the base against the sides of the body with the wrong sides together. Starting at the nose and stitching toward the tail, oversew the sections together. Repeat on the other side, leaving a gap large enough to push the stuffing through.

11 Stuff the hedgehog, then oversew the opening closed.

Try This!

Make a mouse

To transform the hedgehog pattern into a mouse, you can use the same body shape. Fill each side panel with gray fleece, then add little round ears and a pink fleece tail.

Sassy Squirrel

Hiding away nuts for winter, his nose and bushy tail twitching busily among the trees, this fluffy friend also enjoys staying home with you when it's cold outside.

You will need

20 x 20 in. (50 x 50cm) burlap

30 x 20 in. (75 x 50cm) taupe fleece

10 x 10 in. (25 x 25cm) white fleece

2 x 2 in. (5 x 5cm) brown fleece

2 x 2 in. (5 x 5cm) beige fleece

one pair ½-in. (12mm) black safety eyes

10 oz. (250g) polyester soft toy stuffing

black sewing thread

fabric marking pen

scissors

ruler

pointed rag rug tool

sewing needle

fabric glue (optional)

Difficulty rating

Intermediate

Completed size

8½ x 3 x 9½ in. (22 x 7.5 x 24cm)

Prepare the pieces

1 Using the templates on page 111, cut out the tail pieces from burlap and copy the markings. Cut out the body sections, head gusset, base, and ears from taupe fleece. Cut the tummy from white fleece. Cut the remaining taupe fleece into ½ x 2 in. (1.5 x 5cm) strips (see template on page 101).

Hook the tail

2 Fold the burlap for one tail section along the marked lines and use the technique shown on page 103 to secure the fold with strips of taupe fabric. Fill the outline until the folded edge is secure. Use scissors to trim any excess burlap. Repeat for the other burlap tail section.

Make the body

3 Place the two body sections together with the right sides facing each other. Sew the sections together using a backstitch from the chin to the nose (marked A–B on the template), leaving the seam allowance shown on the template. Position the head gusset between the body sections and sew around one side, stopping where the ear will be positioned (marked B–C on the template).

4 Fold one ear in half lengthwise, then position it between the side and head gusset (marked on the template). Make sure the open side of the ear faces toward the nose. Backstitch into position.

5 Repeat steps 1 and 2 to complete the other side of the head and ear. Sew down the back of the squirrel using a backstitch, stopping about 1½ in. (4cm) from the bottom (marked D–E on the template).

Add the tummy

6 Sew the darts where indicated on the white tummy section using a backstitch. (Marked A and F on the template.) Align the smaller dart at the top with the seam in the chin section, then sew down both sides using a backstitch to secure.

Add the eyes

7 Turn the body right side out. Position the eyes as marked on the template and attach them using the technique shown on page 105.

Add the base

8 Align the center of the dart at the bottom of the tummy with the center of the base section (marked F on the template). Oversew around each side from this point. Stuff the squirrel. Oversew the back closed.

Add the tail

9 Hold the two tail sections with the wrong sides facing each other and oversew along the top edge and halfway along the bottom edge, leaving a gap large enough to push the stuffing through. Stuff the tail and oversew the opening closed. Stitch the tail in place on the body. If necessary, use scissors to trim the fleece covering the tail so it is a uniform length.

Make the nut

10 Roll some scraps of fleece into a ball and tie with thread to secure. Cover with a small piece of beige fleece and stitch to create texture (see photograph on page 23). Cut a circle from the brown fleece and add this to the bottom to create the base of the nut. Stitch the nut in position between the upper paws.

Try This!

Red squirrel

Change things up by making a red squirrel. These creatures have longer ears than their gray cousins, so elongate the pattern before you cut the pieces out. The colors of their coats vary with the seasons —from red in the summer to deep brown in the winter—just choose the shade of fleece you prefer.

Farmyard Favorites

The farmer makes sure lamb and pig spend plenty of time in the fields. The duck likes to swim in the farm pond and preen himself at the water's edge. In the evenings, the bat flies out of the barn to eat insects.

Little Lamb

This bouncy spring lamb spends happy days playing with his friends, bleating happily as they frolic in the sun before taking shelter in the barn.

You will need

20 x 10 in. (50 x 25cm) burlap

20 x 20 in. (50 x 50cm) white fleece

20 x 10 in. (50 x 25cm) black fleece

2 x 4 in. (5 x 10cm) brown fleece

one pair ½-in. (12mm) black safety eyes

10 oz. (250g) polyester soft toy stuffing

black and white sewing thread

fabric marking pen

scissors

ruler

pointed rag rug tool

sewing needle

fabric glue (optional)

Difficulty rating

Easy

Completed size

5½ x 7½ x 5½ in. (14 x 19 x 14cm)

Prepare the pieces

1 Using the templates on page 112, cut out the body sections from burlap and copy the markings. Cut out the legs and the top and sides of the head from black fleece as directed on the templates. Cut out the eyes from brown fleece. Cut a ½ x 10 in. (1.5 x 25cm) strip from the black fleece; this will be used to join the head to the body. Cut the white fleece into ½ x 2 in. (1.5 x 5cm) strips (see template on page 101).

Hook the pieces

2 Secure the edges of the burlap body sections with strips of white fleece using the technique shown on page 103. Fill the outline until the edges are secure. Once complete, trim excess burlap using scissors.

3 Fill in the body sections, using white fleece and the technique shown on page 102.

Make the legs

4 Fold one of the leg sections in half lengthwise with the wrong sides together, then backstitch along two sides (marked A–B on the template), leaving the seam allowance shown on the template. Do not stitch the strips that will attach the leg to the body. Turn right side out, then stuff the leg. Repeat with the remaining leg sections.

5 Push the four strips at the base of one of the legs through one side of the body at the point shown on the template, keeping them three strands of burlap apart. Tie the strips together in pairs using a double knot. Secure with fabric glue if desired. Repeat for the other legs.

Make the head

6 Fold the face section in half with the wrong sides together and backstitch around the chin (marked C–D on the template), leaving the seam allowance shown on the template.

7 Cut small holes in the centers of the brown fleece circles. Make small holes in the head for the eyes at the points marked on the template. Attach the fleece circles to the head using the safety eyes and the technique shown on page 105.

8 With the wrong sides facing, align the center of the top of the head (marked E on the template) with the sides and backstitch together as far as the chin (marked D on the template), leaving a gap large enough to turn the head right side out. Fold in the ears so they will stick out when the head is turned right side out.

9 Thread the long strip of black fleece through the two slits in the back of the head panel so the ends protrude from the back. Turn the head right side out, stuff, then oversew the opening closed.

Completing the lamb

10 Hold the body sections with the wrong sides together. Starting at the front legs and stitching toward the neck, oversew the sections together. Stop sewing when you get to the center of the back.

11 Push the ends of the strips of fleece through the sides of the body as close to the sewn edge as possible. Tie the strips together using a double knot. Secure with fabric glue if desired.

12 Continue to oversew the body sections together, leaving a gap between the legs large enough to add the stuffing. Stuff the body, then oversew the opening closed. If necessary, use scissors to trim the fleece covering the body so it is a uniform length, being careful not to cut the ears.

Try This!

Fluffy fleece

Swap out the fleece for natural felting fiber or some sheep's wool to create a super fluffy lamb. You can also try the loop technique shown on page 104.

Pink Pig

You'll usually find this ball of fun splashing in the mud, or with his nose in a mound of acorns and his curly tail wagging. But he'll happily enjoy a cuddle too.

You will need

20 x 20 in. (50 x 50cm) burlap

20 x 40 in. (50 x 100cm) light pink fleece

8 x ¾ in. (20 x 2cm) strip of black fleece

one pair ½-in. (12mm) black safety eyes

one 6-in. (15cm) pipe cleaner

10 oz. (250g) polyester soft toy stuffing

pink sewing thread

fabric marking pen

scissors

ruler

fabric marking pen

pointed rag rug tool

sewing needle

fabric glue (optional)

Difficulty rating

Easy

Completed size

6 x 8 x 3½ in. (15 x 20 x 9cm)

Prepare the pieces

1 Using the templates on page 113, cut out the pieces for the body and base from burlap, copying the markings. Cut out the ears, nose, and tail from the pink fleece. Cut a ½ x 20 in. (1.5 x 50cm) strip from pink fleece; this will be used to secure the underside. Cut the remaining pink fleece into ½ x 2 in. (1.5 x 5cm) strips (see template on page 101). Cut a strip of black fleece measuring ½ x 4¾ in. (1.5 x 12cm) for the nostrils.

Hook the sections

2 Fold the burlap for one of the sides along the marked lines and use the technique shown on page 103 to work around the edge to secure the fold. Fill the outline of the side in the same way. Continue until the folded edge is secure. Once the outline is complete, trim any excess burlap. Repeat the process for the other side.

Add the eyes

3 Attach the eyes as marked on the template using the technique on page 105. Fill in both sides of the pig with strips of pink fleece using the technique on page 102.

Making the base

4 Fold the burlap for the base panel along the marked lines. Use the 20-in. (50cm) strip of pink fleece to secure the edge using the technique shown on page 103.

Add the ears and nose

5 Attach an ear to each side of the body by pushing the strips at the base of the ear through the burlap and tying the strips together on the wrong side using a double knot. Secure with a dab of fabric glue if desired. For clarity, the strips are shown in black in the photograph.

6 Hold the front and back body pieces with the wrong sides together and oversew the two pieces together from the chin to the top of the snout (marked A–B on the template).

7 Cut slits in the nose as shown on the template. Cut the strip of black fleece in half and thread each piece in and out of one set of slits so you have four ends protruding from the back of the nose.

8 To attach the nose to the face, thread the black strips through the burlap, keeping them three strands of burlap apart. Tie the strips together on the wrong side using a double knot. Secure with a dab of fabric glue if desired.

Complete the pig

9 To attach the base panel, align the legs with the legs on the side panels and oversew around the edge of the base (marked B–C on the template).

10 Fold the tail in half lengthwise and sew using a backstitch along the long edge, leaving the seam allowance shown on the template. Turn the tail right side out and insert the pipe cleaner into the center. Trim the end of the pipe cleaner so it is level with the end of the tail.

11 Sew together the back section of the sides (marked A–D on the template), leaving a gap large enough to push the stuffing through (marked D–C on the template). Add the tail by pushing the strips at the base through the burlap, three strands of burlap apart. Tie the strips together on the wrong side using a double knot. Secure the ends with fabric glue if desired.

12 Stuff the pig, then oversew the opening closed. Twist the tail around your finger to give it a curl. The pipe cleaner will help hold the tail's shape. If necessary, use scissors to trim the fleece covering the pig so it is a uniform length.

Try This!

Time for tea

Bring a splash of color to the table with a pig-shaped tea cozy. Scale up the pattern to one and a half or two times the size (see page 100) and omit the base. For added insulation, line the cozy with a layer of fleece.

Spooky Bat

Often out after midnight, especially on Halloween, this flappy black bat enjoys a spooky flight in the crisp night air in the farmyard before coming home to roost.

You will need

10 x 20 in. (25 x 50cm) burlap

20 x 30 in. (50 x 75cm) black fleece

2 x 2 in. (5 x 5cm) brown fleece

four 6-in. (15cm) pipe cleaners

one pair ½-in. (12mm) black safety eyes

10 oz. (250g) polyester soft toy stuffing

black sewing thread

fabric marking pen

scissors

ruler

pointed rag rug tool

sewing needle

fabric glue (optional)

Difficulty rating

intermediate

Completed size

5¼ x 12 x 6¼ in. (13 x 30 x 16cm)

Prepare the pieces

1 Using the templates on page 114, cut out the body sections from burlap and copy the markings. Cut out the wings, ears, and head from black fleece as directed on the templates. Cut eyes from brown fleece. Cut the remaining black fleece into ½ x 2 in. (1.5 x 5cm) strips (see template on page 101).

Hook the pieces

2 Secure the edges of the burlap body sections with strips of black fleece using the technique shown on page 103. Fill the outline until the folded edge is secure. Once the outline is complete, trim any excess burlap using scissors.

3 Fill in the body sections using the technique shown on page 102.

Making the wings

4 Bend one pipe cleaner in half along the edge of one wing as shown in the photograph. Fold the fabric over the pipe cleaner to enclose it and use a running stitch to hold it in place. The fabric should be wrapped around the pipe cleaner as tightly as possible. Repeat for the other wing.

5 Bend a pipe cleaner into a V shape and position it in the center of one of the wings as shown in the photograph. Attach to the wing using the same technique as described in step 4. Repeat for the other wing.

6 Cut lengthwise along the center of the tab on each wing as shown in the photograph to create two strips about 2 in. (5cm) long.

Completing the body

7 Push the two strips at the base of one of the wings through the center of one body section, keeping them three strands of burlap apart. Tie the strips together using a double knot. Secure with fabric glue if desired. Repeat for the other wing on the other side of the body.

8 Hold the body sections with the wrong sides facing. Oversew the sections together, leaving a gap large enough to attach the face. Pink thread is used in the photograph to show the stitches.

Making the head

9 Fold the fleece head section in half lengthwise and backstitch along the curved and long straight edge to create a pocket. Turn the head right side out.

10 Cut a hole in the centers of the brown fleece circles. Position the head over the opening in the body. Position a brown circle on the head and attach it using one of the safety eyes and the technique shown on page 105. This will attach the head to the body. Repeat on the other side of the face. Stuff the body, then oversew the opening closed. Stuff the head if desired.

11 Position the ears on each side of the head and oversew in place. If necessary, use scissors to trim the fleece covering for the body so it is a uniform length.

Try This!

Halloween visitor

Use strips of black plastic bags in place of the fleece to create a super spooky Halloween decoration.

Fluffy Duck

Quacking excitedly as she paddles her flappy feet among the reeds and bobs for pond weed, this fluffy duck will waddle back home to stay with you.

You will need

20 x 20 in. (50 x 50cm) burlap

40 x 20 in. (100 x 50cm) yellow fleece

10 x 8 in. (25 x 20cm) orange fleece

one pair ½-in. (12mm) black safety eyes

10 oz. (250g) polyester soft toy stuffing

yellow and orange sewing thread

fabric marking pen

scissors

ruler

pointed rag rug tool

sewing needle

fabric glue (optional)

Difficulty rating

Intermediate

Completed size

7½ x 4¾ x 4¼ in. (19 x 12 x 11cm)

Prepare the pieces

1 Using the templates on page 115, cut out the body, wing, and tummy sections from burlap and copy the markings. Cut out the bill and feet from orange fleece as directed on the templates. Cut a ½ x 10 in. (1.5 x 25cm) strip from the yellow fleece; this will be used to secure the wings. Cut the remaining yellow fleece into ½ x 2 in. (1.5 x 5cm) strips (see template on page 101).

Hook the pieces

2 Secure the edges of the burlap body sections with strips of yellow fleece using the technique shown on page 103. Fill the outline using strips of fleece as shown on the templates. Continue until the folded edge is secure. Once the outline is complete, trim any excess burlap using scissors. Repeat with the tummy and wing sections.

Add the eyes

3 Position one of the eyes on one of the body sections as marked on the template and attach it using the technique shown on page 105. Repeat on the other side.

4 Fill in the burlap sections using strips of yellow fleece and the technique shown on page 102.

Add the feet

5 Push the four strips at the base of the feet through the tummy at the point shown on the template, keeping them three strands of burlap apart. Tie the strips together using a double knot. Secure with fabric glue if desired.

Add the wings

6 To attach the wings, cut the long strip of yellow fleece in half (black fleece is used in the photographs). Fold one strip in half and push both ends through the tip of one of the wings as shown on the template, then push each end through the body at the point shown on the template.

7 Pull the strip of fabric through the body and tie together in a double knot, adding fabric glue if desired. Repeat for the other wing.

Adding the tummy

8 Hold one of the body sections and the tummy section with the wrong sides together. Starting at the base and stitching toward the head (marked A–B on the template), oversew the sections together. Black thread is used in the photograph to show the stitches. Repeat for the other side.

Making the bill

9 Hold the two bill sections with the wrong sides facing and backstitch together along three sides (marked E–F on the template), leaving a ¼ in. (5mm) seam allowance. Do not stitch the strips that will attach the bill to the body. Black thread is used in the photograph to show the stitches. Turn right side out.

Completing the duck

10 Starting at the point where the tummy joins the sides and stitching toward the head (marked B–C on the template), oversew the side sections together until you reach the point where you need to add the bill.

11 Push the eight strips at the base of the bill through the head at the point shown on the template, keeping them three strands of burlap apart. Tie the strips together in pairs using a double knot. Secure with fabric glue if desired.

12 Oversew the remaining seam (marked A–C on the template), leaving a gap large enough to push the stuffing through. Stuff the duck, then oversew the opening closed. If necessary, use scissors to trim the fleece covering the body so it is a uniform length, being careful not to cut the bill or feet.

Try This!

Feature feathers

Vary the color of the fleece to create different breeds of ducks and add splashes of color or to add a feathery texture to the wings.

Perfect
Pets

If you're looking for a faithful friend,
then a kitten or puppy is likely to
be your pet of choice. The tortoise
appreciates a quiet home and
hibernates all winter. Meanwhile, bunny
enjoys being in the garden and
nibbling on carrots.

Cuddly Kitten

This cute ball of fluff likes nothing more than a game with a ball of string or a scurrying mouse before nuzzling in for a catnap on your lap.

You will need

20 x 20 in. (50 x 50cm) burlap

20 x 40 in. (50 x 100cm) black fleece

10 x 20 in. (25 x 50cm) white fleece

4 x 4 in. (10 x 10cm) pink fleece

one pair ½-in. (12mm) black safety eyes

24 in. (60cm) clear nylon fishing wire

10 oz. (250g) polyester soft toy stuffing

black sewing thread

fabric marking pen

scissors

ruler

pointed rag rug tool

sewing needle

fabric glue (optional)

Difficulty rating

Challenging

Completed size

9⅓ x 5 x 11½ in. (24 x 13 x 29cm)

Preparing the pieces

1 Cut out the sides, front, feet, and tail from burlap, using the templates on page 116, and copy the markings. Cut out the ears from black fleece. Cut a ½ x 10 in. (1.5 x 25cm) strip of black fleece; this will be used to attach the legs. Cut the remaining black fleece and the white fleece into ½ x 2 in. (1.5 x 5cm) strips (see template on page 101).

2 Secure the edges of the burlap shapes using the technique shown on page 103. Fill in the outlines using the colors shown on the templates.

3 Fold the tail in half lengthwise and oversew along the long side (marked A–B on the template). Pink thread is used in the photograph to show the stitches.

Assembling the body

4 Fold one of the feet sections up and around one front leg (marked C–D on the template) and oversew in place. Repeat with the other front leg and foot.

5 Position the front of the body against the sides with the wrong sides together. Oversew from the base to the neck (marked E–F on the template). When you reach the front leg, sew the open side of the burlap so that there will be no open seams when you stuff the kitten. Repeat on the other side.

Adding the features

6 Add the eyes where they are marked on the template and secure using the technique on page 105. To make the whiskers, cut the nylon wire into four equal lengths. Using two lengths of wire on each side of the nose, thread them in and out of the burlap and secure them using double knots.

7 Create the head by sewing the side panels together where they join the front to just past the white section of the nose (marked F–G on the template).

8 Cut out the nose from pink fleece. Secure it to the face using a few small stab stitches.

Adding the ears

9 To add the ears, push the four strips of fabric at the base of one ear through the burlap on one side of the head, keeping them three strands of burlap apart. Tie them together in pairs using double knots at the back. Secure with a dab of fabric glue if desired. Repeat on the other side of the head.

Adding the feet

10 Add the feet to the back legs by cutting the ½ x 10 in. (1.5 x 25cm) strip of black fleece in half (shown in yellow in the photograph). Thread one piece through the center of one of the feet where it's marked on the template. The ends of the strip should be pushed through, keeping them three strands of burlap apart. Repeat for the other side.

11 Push the ends of the strip through the side panel where it's marked on the template. Make sure the two ends of the strip are three strands of burlap apart and secure with a double knot. Repeat for the other side.

Completing the kitten

12 Sew together the two sides from the head to the base (marked G–H on the template), adding the tail as you go (marked A–A on the template). Stuff your cat, then oversew the base to close the opening (marked E–H on the template). If necessary, use scissors to trim the fleece covering the cat so it is a uniform length.

Try This!

Fluffy kitten

To make a truly furry kitten, use a natural felting fiber or wool rather than fleece to make the fur. The result will be a super fluffy finish. You may also want to try the loop stitch shown on page 104.

Darling Puppy

With floppy ears and a wagging tail, big eyes, and a happy smile, every puppy is adorable. And this little fellow won't chew your slippers.

You will need

20 x 20 in. (50 x 50cm) burlap

20 x 40 in. (50 x 100cm) beige fleece

one pair ½-in. (12mm) black safety eyes

one ½-in. (12mm) black safety nose

10 oz. (250g) polyester soft toy stuffing

beige sewing thread

fabric marking pen

scissors

ruler

pointed rag rug tool

sewing needle

fabric glue (optional)

Difficulty rating

Intermediate

Completed size

7 x 9 x 5 in. (18 x 23 x 12cm)

Prepare the pieces

1 Cut out the body, base, and chin from burlap, using the templates on page 117, and copy the markings. Cut out the ears and tail from the beige fleece. Cut the remaining fleece into ½ x 2 in. (1.5 x 5cm) strips (see template on page 101).

2 Secure the edges of the burlap body sections using the technique shown on page 103. Fill in the outline of the body, followed by the base and chin sections. Trim any excess burlap using scissors.

Add the eyes

3 Secure the eyes in the positions shown on the templates using the technique shown on page 105. Fill in all the sections using the technique shown on page 102.

Start to assemble the body

4 Line up one side of the body with the muzzle, then oversew together using a needle and beige thread (marked A–B on the template). Pink thread is used in the photographs to show the stitches. Repeat the process for the other side section.

Complete the body

7 Align the legs on the base section with the legs on one of the side panels and oversew the sections together, starting at the chin and ending at the tail (marked C–D on the template).

8 Repeat for the other side of the base section. If the legs splay when you stand the dog up, remove a few pieces of fleece from the center of the base.

Complete the head

5 Push the four strips at the base of one of the ears through the burlap on one side of the head, about three strands of burlap apart, and use double knots to tie the strips together in pairs at the back. Secure with a dab of fabric glue if desired. Repeat on the second side.

6 Use a sewing needle and beige thread to sew together the front of the head by oversewing from the point where the central head and two side panels join to the chin (marked A–C on the template). Push the nose through a gap in the stitching and secure in the same way as the eyes.

Add the tail

9 Fold the tail in half, with the right sides facing, and use a backstitch to sew from the tip to the point where the strips begin (marked F–G on the template), leaving the seam allowance shown on the template. Turn right side out.

10 Oversew the side and base panels together to join the base of the back (marked D–E on the template), leaving a gap large enough to push the stuffing through (marked B–E on the template). Add the tail by pushing the strips at the base through the burlap, making sure the seam runs down the center of the tail and the strips are three strands of burlap apart. Use double knots to tie the strips of fabric together and secure with a dab of fabric glue if desired.

Finish your puppy

11 Stuff the puppy and oversew the remaining open seams closed. If necessary, use scissors to trim the fleece covering the puppy so it is a uniform length, being careful not to cut the ears or the tail.

Try This!

Proggy portrait

Create a proggy version of your own pup by choosing fabrics that match his coat and adding stripes or patches as necessary.

Floppy Bunny

This bunny's big ears are listening for the farmer; his eyes are alert and his nose is twitching. He'll mischievously nibble the crops and then hop home with his white tail bobbing.

You will need

20 x 20 in. (50 x 50cm) burlap

20 x 40 in. (50 x 100cm) white fleece

6 x 6 in. (15 x 15cm) pink fleece

one pair ½-in. (12mm) black safety eyes

10 oz. (250g) polyester soft toy stuffing

white sewing thread

fabric marking pen

scissors

ruler

pointed rag rug tool

sewing needle

fabric glue (optional)

Difficulty rating

Intermediate

Completed size

8 x 5 x 4 in. (20 x 13 x 10cm)

Prepare the pieces

1 Using the templates on page 118, cut out the sides and base from burlap, copying the markings. Cut out the tail, nose, and ears from the white and pink fleece as directed. Cut the remaining white fleece into ½ x 2 in. (1.5 x 5cm) strips (see template on page 101).

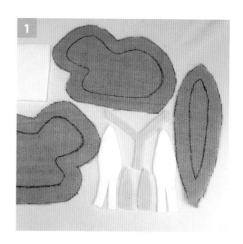

Hook the edges

2 Fold the burlap for one of the sides along the solid marked template lines and use the technique shown on page 103 to secure the fold. Continue until the folded edge is secure. Once the outline is complete, trim any excess burlap using scissors. Repeat the process for the second side and the base.

Add the eyes

3 Insert the safety eyes in the positions marked on the template using the technique shown on page 105.

Assemble the tail

4 Place a ball of stuffing in the center of the tail section. Fold two corners over the stuffing diagonally to make a tube and stitch the corners together. Repeat with the second pair of corners.

5 Continue to bring the edges of the fabric together and secure with stitches until you have a round tail. Secure the thread, but do not cut it, as you will use it to sew the tail to the body.

Assemble the ears

6 Use white thread to sew the pink inner ears to the centers of the larger white ears using a stab stitch. If you don't want to sew them, you can attach them with a dab of fabric glue.

7 Push the strips at the base of one ear through the body panel as marked on the template. Position the strips about three strands of burlap apart and tie them together using a double knot. Add a dab of fabric glue to secure if desired. Repeat for the other ear.

Complete the body

8 Fill in the rest of the panels using the technique shown on page 102.

9 Position the base against the side pieces with right sides facing out and oversew together from the feet to the tail (marked A–B on the template) along both sides.

10 Sew from where the base joins the sides to the top of the head. Stop at the top of the head (marked A–C on the template) so there is space to add the nose.

Add the nose

11 Push the strips at the end of the Y-shaped nose piece into the burlap using the same technique as for the ears. When you are happy with the position, tie the strips together on the inside to secure using double knots.

12 Oversew the body from the head to the tail, leaving a gap large enough to push the stuffing through (marked B–C on the template). Stuff the rabbit, then sew up the opening. Stitch the tail into position. If necessary, use scissors to trim the fleece so it is a uniform length.

Try This!

Pose-able ears

To make the rabbit's ears more expressive, cut out two white shapes for each ear and sew them together before inserting a pipe cleaner into each one (like the pig's tail on page 35). Then you can position the ears in a floppy pose.

Tiny Tortoise

Slow and steady wins the race they say. This little guy has the life of Riley lounging in the summer sunshine and sleeping through the winter in his pretty patterned shell.

You will need

10 x 20 in. (25 x 50cm) burlap

20 x 15 in. (50 x 40cm) bright green fleece

20 x 15 in. (50 x 40cm) dark green fleece

one pair ½-in. (12mm) black safety eyes

10 oz. (250g) polyester soft toy stuffing

green sewing thread

scissors

ruler

pointed rag rug tool

sewing needle

seam ripper (optional)

Difficulty rating

Intermediate

Completed size

3 x 8 x 5 in. (8 x 20 x 12cm)

Prepare the pieces

1 Using the templates on page 119, cut out the shell and base sections from burlap and copy the markings. Cut out the legs and head from dark green fleece as directed on the templates. Cut a ½ x 10 in. (1.5 x 25cm) strip from the dark green fleece; this will be used to secure the edges of the base of the shell. Cut the remaining dark green and bright green fleece into ½ x 2 in. (1.5 x 5cm) strips (see template on page 101).

Make the legs

2 With the right sides facing, use a backstitch to sew one of the leg sections together, leaving the seam allowance shown on the template. Do not sew together the strips as you will need to use them to attach the legs to the body. Turn the leg right side out and stuff. Repeat with the remaining leg pieces.

Make the head

3 With right sides facing, use a backstitch to sew the two head sections together along the curved edges, leaving the seam allowance shown on the template. Yellow thread is used in the photographs to show the stitches.

4 Decide where you want to place the eyes and make small holes with scissors or a seam ripper. Attach one of the safety eyes using the technique shown on page 105. Repeat on the other side. Turn the head right side out and stuff.

Make the shell base

5 To secure the edges of the burlap shell base section, use the long strip of dark green fleece to create a running stitch around the folded edge using the technique shown on page 103. Once the outline is complete, trim any excess burlap using scissors.

6 Decide on the placement of the legs around the base. Push the strips from the base of one leg through one side of the shell base, keeping the strips three strands of burlap apart. Tie the strips together using a double knot. Secure with fabric glue if desired. Repeat for the other legs.

Make the shell

7 Secure the edges of the burlap shell section with strips of dark green fleece using the technique shown on page 103. Fill the outline using strips of bright green fleece as shown on the templates. Once the outline is complete, trim any excess burlap using scissors. Fill the lines on the shell with dark green fleece and the spaces between them with bright green fleece using the technique shown on page 102 to complete the shell.

Complete the turtle

8 Use stab stitches to attach the head to one end of the shell.

9 Hold the shell sections with the wrong sides facing and oversew together, leaving a gap large enough to push the stuffing through. Sew through the ends of the legs, but take care not to catch the fabric covering the shell in the stitches.

10 Stuff the shell, then oversew the opening closed. If necessary, use scissors to trim the fleece covering the shell so it is a uniform length.

Try This!

Shell effects

Working the shell in faux leather will give your tortoise shell a great texture. Another fantastic alternative is using a printed fleece, which will produce some interesting patterns on the shell.

Feathered
Friends

The plumage of these birds recalls
their diverse homes. The parrot's
bright feathers could only belong
in a tropical country, while the baby
penguin's gray covering is perfect
for an icy destination. The coloring
of the robin and owl help camouflage
them in woods and fields.

Pretty Parrot

This tropical bird loves to talk. His colorful plumage and fluffy feathers mean he looks equally at home perched on a pirate's shoulder or brightening up your house.

You will need

20 x 20 in. (50 x 50cm) burlap

10 x 10 in. (25 x 25cm) blue fleece

10 x 8 in. (25 x 20cm) yellow fleece

10 x 8 in. (25 x 20cm) white fleece

10 x 8 in. (25 x 20cm) black fleece

one pair ½-in. (12mm) black safety eyes

10 oz. (250g) polyester soft toy stuffing

white, blue, and yellow sewing thread

fabric marking pen

scissors

ruler

pointed rag rug tool

sewing needle

fabric glue (optional)

Difficulty rating
Challenging

Completed size
15 x 4 x 5 in. (38 x 10 x 13cm)

Prepare the pieces

1 Cut out the body and wings from burlap using the templates on page 120 and copy the markings. Cut out the eyes, tail, and beak from the black, white, blue, and yellow fleece as indicated on the templates. Cut a ½ x 10 in. (1.5 x 25cm) strip from the blue fleece; this will be used to attach the wings. Cut the remaining blue and yellow fleece into ½ x 2 in. (1.5 x 5cm) strips (see template on page 101).

Assemble the face

2 Use the tip of a pair of scissors to make a hole for the eye in each of the white face sections. Position the face sections onto the burlap body sections and attach using small running stitches with white thread. Attach the safety eyes to the face sections, inserting them through the holes and using the technique shown on page 105.

Hook the edges

3 Fold the burlap for one of the body sections along the solid marked lines and use the technique shown on page 103 to secure the fold with strips of blue fleece. Repeat for the second body section and the wings using blue and yellow fleece as indicated on the templates. Fill in all the pieces using the technique shown on page 102.

Make the tail and beak

4 Layer the three tail sections so the longest piece is at the bottom and the shortest is at the top. Use blue thread and a needle to tack the three layers together ¼ in. (5mm) from the straight edge.

5 Arrange the beak sections as shown in the photograph. Sew them together using a backstitch and a ¼ in. (5mm) seam allowance in the order below, bending the black diamond to fit the contours of the white pieces, and create the shape of the beak. Using the lettering on the templates, sew together A–B, B–C, A–D, C–D, A–E, and C–F.

6 When all four beak sections are attached to the central section, sew the two white sections together using a backstitch and leaving the seam allowance shown on the template, then sew the black sections together. Turn the beak right side out.

Attach the wings

7 Cut the long strip of blue fleece in half (yellow fabric is used in the photograph for clarity). Fold one strip in half and push both ends through the tip of one of the wings as indicated on the template, then push each end through the body at the point marked on the template.

8 Pull the strip of fabric through the body and tie the ends together in a double knot, adding a dab of fabric glue to secure if desired. Repeat for the other wing.

Complete the parrot

9 Oversew the beak to the body sections using white thread. Align the beak with the face and start sewing at the top of the beak, where the two white sections meet, down to the center of the black section.

10 Using blue thread, join the body sections in the same way, starting at the beak and oversewing over the top of the head and down the back of the body to the tail. Align the center of the tail with the point where the two back sections meet; stitch in place leaving a gap large enough to push the stuffing through.

11 Stuff the parrot, then oversew the open seam from the tummy to the tail. If necessary, use scissors to trim the fleece covering the parrot so it is a uniform length.

Try This!

Cotton feathers

This project works really well using scraps of cotton instead of fleece; it will fray slightly and give your parrot a more feathery look.

Wise Old Owl

This wise old owl is a real hoot! He certainly knows a thing or two about flying at night and sleeping all day—he'd rather snooze with you.

You will need

20 x 20 in. (50 x 50cm) burlap

20 x 40 in. (50 x 100cm) leopard print fleece (any brown pattern will do)

10 x 10 in. (25 x 25cm) beige fleece

8 x 4 in. (20 x 10cm) yellow fleece

6 x 3 in. (15 x 8cm) white fleece

one pair ½-in. (12mm) black safety eyes

10 oz. (250g) polyester soft toy stuffing

black or brown sewing thread

fabric marking pen

pointed rag rug tool

sewing needle

fabric glue (optional)

Difficulty rating

Easy

Completed size

7 x 6 x 3½ in. (18 x 15 x 9cm)

Prepare the pieces

1 Using the templates on page 121, cut out the body and wings from burlap, copying the markings.

2 Cut out the eyes and beak from the yellow fleece as directed. Cut out the inner eyes from the white fleece. Cut out the ears from the leopard print fleece, along with a ½ x 10 in. (1.5 x 25cm) strip that will be used to attach the wings. Cut the remaining leopard print and beige fabric into ½ x 2 in. (1.5 x 5cm) strips (see template on page 101).

Hooking the edges

3 Fold the burlap for one of the sides along the solid marked template lines. Use the technique shown on page 103 to secure the folded edge.

4 Continue until the folded edge is secure. Once the outline is complete, trim any excess burlap using scissors. Repeat the process for the back and the wings.

Adding the features

5 To add the eyes, fold the white circles in half and then in half again. Snip a tiny piece from the center point. Repeat with the yellow circles and align the holes. Alternatively, you may prefer to position the holes off-center to change your owl's expression. Insert the safety eyes through the felt and burlap in the position marked on the template.

6 Secure the eyes using the technique shown on page 105, but don't make them too tight (just the first notch will be enough).

7 To add the beak, push each side of the yellow beak section through the burlap as indicated on the template. The two strips should be three strands of burlap apart. Tie the two sections in a double knot at the back. If desired, add a dab of fabric glue to secure the knot.

8 Attach the ears at the top of the head on the front using the same technique for attaching the beak. Insert in the positions marked on the template.

Finishing

9 Fill in the centers of the front, back, and wings of the owl using the technique shown on page 102. Remember to fill in the tummy section with the beige and leave gaps around the eyes.

10 Join the front and back of the owl by oversewing the two sides together. For clarity, blue thread is used in the photograph.

11 To attach the wings, take half of the long leopard print strip you kept to one side (for clarity, a gray strip is used in the photograph). Loop both ends through the wing, and then use the rag rug tool to push each end into the body where it begins to widen after the head.

12 Pull the strip of fabric through the body, then tie together with a double knot, adding fabric glue if desired. Repeat for the other wing, then finish sewing up the side. Partially sew on the base, leaving a gap large enough to push the stuffing through. Stuff the owl, then oversew the open seam. If necessary, use scissors to trim the fleece covering the owl so it is a uniform length.

Try This!

Glove puppet

Leave off the base panel and don't stuff your owl in order to create a puppet. To create a snowy owl, use white fleece for the whole body.

Rockin' Robin

We may associate him with Christmas, but thanks to his natural curiosity, the little red-breasted friend will hop straight into your heart and stay there all year.

You will need

20 x 20 in. (50 x 50cm) burlap

30 x 20 in. (75 x 50cm) dark brown fleece

10 x 10 in. (25 x 25cm) red fleece

10 x 8 in. (25 x 20cm) white fleece

4 x 4 in. (10 x 10cm) yellow fleece

one pair ½-in. (12mm) black safety eyes

10 oz. (250g) polyester soft toy stuffing

black sewing thread

fabric marking pen

scissors

ruler

pointed rag rug tool

sewing needle

fabric glue (optional)

Difficulty rating

Intermediate

Completed size

7 x 6 x 5 in. (18 x 15 x 13cm)

Prepare the pieces

1 Using the templates on page 122, cut out the body, chest, and wing pieces from burlap, copying the markings. Cut out the beak from yellow fleece. Cut a ½ x 4¾ in. (1.5 x 12cm) strip of yellow fleece; this will be used to attach the beak. Cut two ½ x 4¾ in. (1.5 x 12cm) strips of brown fleece; these will be used to attach the wings. Cut the remaining brown, red, and white fleece into ½ x 2 in. (1.5 x 5cm) strips (see template on page 101).

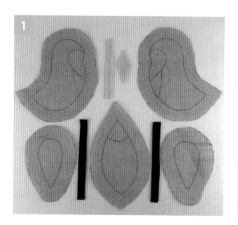

Hook the edges

2 Fold the burlap for one body section along the marked lines and use the technique shown on page 103 to work around the edge to secure the fold. Fill the outline of the body section using dark brown fleece, red for the face, and white for the chest. Continue until the folded edge is secure. Use scissors to trim any excess burlap. Repeat for the other pieces of burlap. Use dark brown fleece for the wings and red and white for the chest.

Add the eyes

3 Secure the safety eyes to the body sections in the positions marked on the template using the technique on page 105. Fill in all the burlap sections with strips of fleece following the colors shown on the templates and using the technique on page 102.

Add the wings

4 To attach the wings, fold one of the long brown strips in half and push both ends through the narrow tip of one of the wings. Yellow fleece is used in the photograph for clarity.

5 Push both ends through the body at the point where it begins to widen after the head and about three strands of burlap apart. Pull the strip of fabric through the body, pull tight, then tie the ends together in a double knot, adding a dab of fabric glue to secure if desired. Repeat for the other wing.

Add the chest and beak

6 Starting at the tail end of the body, oversew the chest panel into position along the line marked A–B on the template. Stop when you reach the head, then sew the other side from the tail to the head.

7 Cut along the two lines marked on the beak template and thread the strip of yellow fleece through them. Push the ends of the strip into the burlap. When you are happy with the position of the beak, tie the ends together in a double knot and secure with fabric glue if desired.

Completing the robin

8 Oversew the sides together. A contrasting color thread is used in the photograph to show the stitches. Hold the wrong sides of the pieces together and start at the point where the chest joins the sides, working to the top of the head (marked B–C on the template).

9 Sew the last section, from the head to the tail, leaving a gap large enough to push the stuffing through (marked A–C on the template). Stuff the robin, then oversew the open seam. If necessary, use scissors to trim the fleece covering the robin so it is a uniform length.

Try This!

Set of bowling pins

Create a set of bowling pins by making six robins and adding a weight, such as a bag of rice, inside the base of each one before sewing it up. Thanks to the stuffing, your bowling pins will land softly every time they're knocked over.

Baby Penguin

Although this adorable baby penguin enjoys waddling about in the ice and snow, he loves nothing better than to get out of the cold and stay inside where it's warm.

You will need

20 x 20 in. (50 x 50cm) burlap

30 x 20 in. (75 x 50cm) gray fleece

20 x 10 in. (50 x 25cm) black fleece

8 x 8 in. (20 x 20cm) white fleece

10 oz. (250g) polyester soft toy stuffing

gray sewing thread

fabric marking pen

scissors

ruler

pointed rag rug tool

sewing needle

fabric glue (optional)

Difficulty rating

Easy

Completed size

8 x 5 x 4 in. (20 x 13 x 10cm)

Prepare the pieces

1 Using the templates on page 123, cut out the body, base, and wings from the burlap, copying the markings. Cut a ½ x 4¾ in. (1.5 x 12cm) strip of black fleece for the eyes. Cut out the beak and feet from the black fleece. Cut a ½ x 10 in. (1.5 x 25cm) strip from the gray fleece; this will be used to attach the wings. Cut the remaining gray, black, and white fleece into ½ x 2 in. (1.5 x 5cm) strips (see template on page 101).

Hook the body, wings, and base

2 Fold the burlap for the front along the solid marked template lines and use the technique shown on page 103 to work around the edge to secure the fold. Fill the outline of the body in gray and the outline of the head in black. Continue until the folded edge is secure. Once the outline is complete, trim any excess burlap using scissors. Repeat the outlining process for the back, wings, and base.

Add the features

3 Using the eye positions marked from the back through to the front of the long black strip of fleece from the back through to the front of each eye and tie a double knot. Push the ends back through to the other side three strands of burlap from the first holes and secure with another double knot. Add a dab of fabric glue to secure if desired.

4 Add the beak in the same way as the eyes, pushing through the two strips at the base of the beak from the back to the front. The gap between the strips should be three strands of burlap apart. Tie the strips together at the back with a double knot to secure and add a dab of fabric glue to secure if desired.

Add the feet and wings

5 Attach the feet at the base of the front, pushing the four strips of fleece through the burlap from front to back and tying the pairs together in double knots to secure. Add a dab of fabric glue to secure if desired.

6 Fill in the centers of the front, back, wings, and base using the technique on page 102.

7 Place the front and back pieces together with the wrong sides facing. Starting at the bottom, oversew the two pieces together. Stop about three-quarters of the way around so you can still get your hand inside the body.

8 To attach the wings, cut the long strip of gray fabric in half (leopard print is used in the photograph). Fold one strip in half and push both ends through the tip of one of the wings as shown on the template, then push each end through the body at the point where it begins to widen after the head.

9 Pull the strip of fabric through the body and tie it together in a double knot as before. Secure with fabric glue if desired. Repeat for the other wing. Sew the rest of the front and back together. If you want to stuff your penguin, partially oversew the base to the body, leaving a gap large enough to push the stuffing through, then fill it with the stuffing. Oversew the opening closed. If necessary, use scissors to trim the fleece covering the penguin so it is a uniform length.

Try This!

Doorstop

Fill your penguin with rice or dried beans instead of polyester stuffing to make a friendly doorstop.

Water
Babies

Whether you're on the beach or exploring a garden pond, there's plenty of wildlife to be found. The turtle and clown fish make their homes in warmer waters, while the seal lives in cooler climes. If you're lucky, you may find a frog sitting on a lily pad.

Cute Clown Fish

The stripy clown fish spends his days swimming around the coral reef and hiding in anemones, but he'll gladly take the plunge and come live with you.

You will need

20 x 20 in. (50 x 50cm) burlap

20 x 20 in. (50 x 50cm) orange fleece

20 x 10 in. (50 x 25cm) white fleece

10 x 10 in. (25 x 25cm) black fleece

one pair ½-in. (12mm) black safety eyes

10 oz. (250g) polyester soft toy stuffing

black or white sewing thread

fabric marking pen

scissors

ruler

pointed rag rug tool

sewing needle

fabric glue (optional)

Difficulty rating

intermediate

Completed size

5½ x 10 x 4 in. (14 x 25 x 10cm)

Prepare the pieces

1 Using the templates on page 124, cut out the body sections from burlap and copy the markings. Cut out the fins from orange fleece as directed on the templates. Cut the eyes from white fleece. Cut the remaining orange, white, and black fleece into ½ x 2 in. (1.5 x 5cm) strips (see template on page 101).

Hook the pieces

2 Secure the edges of the burlap body sections with strips of black fleece at the points where the orange and white sections join using the technique shown on page 103. Fill the outline using strips of orange and white fleece as shown on the templates. Continue until the folded edge is secure. Once the outline is complete, trim any excess burlap using scissors.

3 Fill in the black lines using the technique shown on page 102. Then fill in the orange and white sections of the body using the technique shown on page 102. Do not fill in the face. Repeat for the other side.

Completing the face

4 Make a hole in the center of one of the white fleece eyes. Position it on the face section and attach it using one of the safety eyes and the technique shown on page 105. Repeat on the other side. Fill in the face using strips of orange fleece.

Adding the fins

5 Push the two strips at the base of the side fins through one side of the body at the points marked D and E on the template, keeping them three strands of burlap apart. Tie the strips together using a double knot. Secure with fabric glue if desired. Repeat on the other side.

6 Attach the two top fins and the tail fin to one side of the body at the points marked A, B, and C on the template, positioning them close to the edge so they will be in the center of the body when the sides are sewn together.

Completing the fish

7 Hold the body sections with wrong sides facing and stripes aligned. Starting at the chin and stitching toward the tail, start to oversew the sections together.

8 When you reach the fin, hold it to one side and continue sewing until you have sewn past the tail, leaving a gap large enough to push the stuffing through.

9 Stuff the fish, then oversew the opening closed. If necessary, use scissors to trim the fleece covering the fish body so it is a uniform length, being careful not to cut the fins.

Try This!

Creating scales

For a scaly effect, round off the edges of the strips of fleece. You can increase the effect by using different materials for each of the stripes to create more texture.

Snuggly Seal

Twitching his whiskers and eager to play, diving for fish and flapping his flippers for fun, this friendly baby seal will swim and splash his way into your heart.

You will need

18 x 18 in. (45 x 45cm) burlap

40 x 18 in. (100 x 45cm) gray fleece

24 in. (60cm) black nylon fishing line

one pair ½-in. (12mm) black safety eyes

one ½-in. (12mm) black safety nose

10 oz. (250g) polyester soft toy stuffing

gray sewing thread

fabric marking pen

scissors

ruler

pointed rag rug tool

sewing needle

fabric glue (optional)

Difficulty rating

Intermediate

Completed size

6 x 10 x 6 in. (15 x 25 x 15cm)

Prepare the pieces

1 Using the templates on page 125, cut out the body, tummy, and back of the head sections from burlap and copy the markings. Cut out the flippers and tail from gray fleece as directed on the templates. Cut the remaining fleece into ½ x 2 in. (1.5 x 5cm) strips (see template on page 101).

Hook the pieces

2 Secure the edges of the burlap body, tummy, and head sections with gray fleece using the technique shown on page 103. Fill the outline until the folded edge is secure. Once the outline is complete, trim any excess burlap using scissors.

3 Fill in the body, tummy, and head sections using the technique shown on page 102.

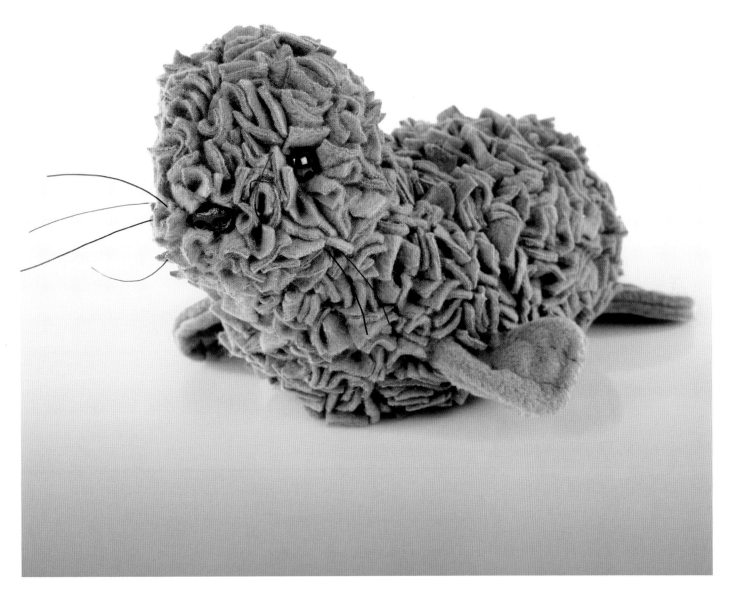

Make the flippers and tail

4 Hold two flipper sections with the wrong sides facing and backstitch together, leaving the seam allowance shown on the template. Do not stitch the strips that will attach the flippers to the body. Repeat with the remaining flipper sections and the tail.

5 Turn the flippers and tail right side out and use a backstitch to mark the details on the flippers and tail. Cut into the fabric to make the joining strips as marked on the template.

6 Push the two strips at the base of the tail into the wider end of the tummy section at the point shown on the template, keeping them three strands of burlap apart. Tie the strips together using a double knot. Secure with fabric glue if desired.

7 Attach the flippers to the sides of the body as marked on the template in the same way.

Add the eyes and whiskers

8 Attach one of the safety eyes to one of the body sections as marked on the template using the technique shown on page 105. Repeat on the other side.

9 Cut the black nylon fishing line into four equal lengths. Thread one length through the seal's nose. Repeat with the other lengths, then tie the wires together in pairs using a double knot.

Completing the seal

10 Hold the body sections with the wrong sides facing. Starting at the back of the head and stitching toward the chin (marked A–B–C on the template), oversew the sections together. Leave a gap in the stitching at the nose to allow for the black plastic nose. Yellow thread is used in the photograph to show the stitches.

11 Attach the safety nose in the gap in the stitching using the technique shown on page 105.

12 Continue sewing the body together working toward the flipper (marked C–D on the template). Position the tummy section and oversew one side until you reach the tail (marked D–E on the template). Repeat on the other side. Oversew the remaining seam, from the head to the tail, leaving a gap large enough to push the stuffing through (marked A–E on the template).

13 Stuff the seal, then oversew the opening closed. If necessary, use scissors to trim the fleece covering the body so it is a uniform length, being careful not to cut the whiskers, flippers, or tail.

Try This!

Make a walrus

To make a walrus, use brown fleece to cover the body, rather than gray, and add a pair of impressive tusks made from white fleece.

Flappy Turtle

With a perfectly patterned shell, this sea-dwelling creature loves to swim, sunbathe, and dive into tropical waters. He will joyfully paddle his way into your life.

You will need

10 x 18 in. (25 x 45cm) burlap

18 x 18 in. (45 x 45cm) bright green fleece

10 x 18 in. (25 x 45cm) taupe fleece

one pair ½-in. (12mm) black safety eyes

10 oz. (250g) polyester soft toy stuffing

green sewing thread

fabric marking pen

scissors

ruler

pointed rag rug tool

sewing needle

seam ripper (optional)

Difficulty rating

Intermediate

Completed size

2¾ x 11 x 12½ in. (7 x 28 x 32cm)

Prepare the pieces

1 Using the templates on page 126, cut out the shell and base sections from burlap and copy the markings. Cut out the chin, flippers, and head from bright green fleece as directed on the templates. Cut a ½ x 10 in. (1.5 x 25cm) strip from the taupe fleece; this will be used to secure the edges of the base of the shell. Cut the remaining bright green and taupe fleece into ½ x 2 in. (1.5 x 5cm) strips (see template on page 101).

Make the flippers

2 With the right sides facing, use a backstitch to sew two of the back flipper sections together, leaving the seam allowance shown on the template. Do not sew together the strips at the end of the flipper, as you will use these to attach the flipper to the body. Turn the flipper section right side out. Repeat with the remaining back flipper pieces.

3 Join the front flipper sections using the same technique as above.

Make the head

4 Sew the head sections together from the nose to the neck (marked A–B on the template) using the same technique as the flippers. Insert the chin (marked A–C and A–D on the template), leaving a gap to push the stuffing through.

5 Make a small hole with a pair of scissors or seam ripper for each eye. Attach using the technique shown on page 105. Turn the head right side out and stuff.

Make the shell base

6 To secure the edges of the burlap shell base section, use the long strip of taupe fleece to create a running stitch around the folded edge using the technique shown on page 103.

7 Decide on the placement for the flippers. Push the strips from the end of one flipper through the shell base, making sure they point toward the tail end, and keep them three strands of burlap apart. Tie the strips together using a double knot. Secure with fabric glue if desired. Repeat for the other flippers.

Make the shell

8 Secure the edges of the burlap shell section with strips of bright green fleece on the marked lines using the technique shown on page 103. Fill the outline using strips of taupe fleece as shown on the templates. Once the outline is complete, trim any excess burlap using scissors.

9 Fill the lines on the shell with bright green fleece and fill the spaces between them with taupe fleece using the technique shown on page 102 to complete the shell.

Complete the turtle

10 Use stab stitches to attach the head to the front end of the shell.

11 Hold the shell sections with the wrong sides facing and oversew them together, leaving a gap large enough to push the stuffing through. Sew through the ends of the flippers, but take care not to catch the fabric covering the shell.

12 Stuff the shell, then oversew the opening closed. If necessary, use scissors to trim the fleece covering so it is a uniform length.

Try This!

Cozy friend

The turtle's shell makes a great hot water bottle cover. Scale up the pattern so the shell will hold your hot water bottle and leave an opening at the head or tail to slide the bottle in.

Crazy Frog

Happily hopping from lily pad to lily pad, this crazy frog makes croaky conversation with his froggy friends about all the adventures he'll have with you.

You will need

10 x 18 in. (25 x 45cm) burlap

18 x 18 in. (45 x 45cm) green fleece

10 x 10 in. (25 x 25cm) 12mm plastic mesh

1 pair ½-in. (12mm) black and green safety eyes

10 oz. (250g) polyester soft toy stuffing

green sewing thread

fabric marking pen

scissors

ruler

pointed rag rug tool

sewing needle

fabric glue (optional)

Difficulty rating

Challenging

Completed size

6¼ x 3½ x 6¼ in. (16 x 9 x 16cm)

Prepare the pieces

1 Using the templates on page 127, cut out the body sections from burlap and copy the markings. Cut out the legs from plastic mesh as directed on the templates. Cut the feet from green fleece. Cut two ½ x 15 in. (1.5 x 38cm) strips from the green fleece; these will be used to secure the edges of the face sections. Cut the remaining green fleece into ½ x 2 in. (1.5 x 5cm) strips (see template on page 101).

2 To secure the edges of one of the burlap body sections, use the long strip of green fleece to create a running stitch around the folded edge using the technique shown on page 103. This will be the base of the body.

Hook the top of the body

3 Secure the edges of the second burlap body section with strips of green fleece using the technique shown on page 103. Fill the outline until the folded edge is secure. Once the outline is complete, trim any excess burlap using scissors. Fill in this body section with strips of green fleece using the technique shown on page 102. Trim any excess burlap using scissors. This will be the top of the body.

Make the legs

4 Cut the remaining strips of green fleece into quarters to make strips small enough to fill the plastic mesh.

5 Use the small pieces of fleece to fill the leg sections using the technique shown for burlap on page 102. Take care not to tear the mesh when using the tool. Fill every hole.

6 Push the two strips at the base of one of the feet through two holes in the mesh. Tie the strips together using a double knot. Secure with fabric glue if desired. Repeat for the other feet.

7 Trim the excess mesh from the edges of the legs. Take care not to cut too close to the fleece strips or the mesh will not hold them in place.

8 Use scissors to trim the fleece covering the legs so it is a uniform length, being careful not to cut the feet.

Completing the frog

9 Position the eyes on the head section of the body and attach using the technique shown on page 105.

10 Hold the body sections with the wrong sides facing. Oversew the head section from shoulder to shoulder. Pink thread is used in the photograph to show the stitches.

11 Continue to oversew the body sections together, adding the legs as you work by stitching through the body and the leg at the same time. Make sure you use three or four stitches for each leg so they are securely attached. Stop when you have a gap just large enough to push the stuffing through.

12 Stuff the body, then oversew the opening closed. If necessary, use scissors to trim the fleece covering for the body so it is a uniform length, being careful not to cut the legs or feet.

Try This!

Recycled bags

Thin plastic is a fantastic alternative material to cover the frog's legs and body. Look for plastic grocery bags in greens and browns; you can even mix in brighter colors to give your frog spots or stripes.

Tools

The proggy technique began as a way to recycle materials using everyday equipment, but there are some tools that will make it easier.

To push the strips of fabric through the burlap base you need a pointed instrument known as a proggy tool. Traditionally, these are made from turned wood, but if you cannot find one you can use a pencil or even a ballpoint pen that has run out of ink.

You can cut the fabric strips using a pair of scissors—a sharp pair will cut through the fabric faster than a blunt pair. You can also use a rotary cutter and cutting board (which are often used to cut fabric for quilting). The board provides a safe surface for the cutting tool, and the grid markings on it will make cutting strips the same width a snap. A dedicated strip cutter board is another useful tool that will make cutting strips easy.

To speed up the process even more, you can buy a special strip snip tool, which turns the long strips into shorter ones that are all the same length. To use it, wind a long fabric strip around the tool, and then cut through the central gap to create uniform lengths of fabric. Having pieces the same length will help reduce the need to trim your proggy animal when you've finished it.

Proggy Tool

Rotary Cutter and Board

Strip Cutter

Strip Snip

Assemble all the tools and materials you need before you begin a project.

Materials

The instructions for each animal include a list of the materials and equipment you will need. Make sure you have them before you begin.

Burlap

The strips of fabric for the fur or feathers are hooked onto burlap. Choose a medium-weight burlap—the weave of a lightweight burlap will be too loose to hold the fabric strips in place, and a heavyweight one will be too tight.

Fleece

Fleece is used to cover the burlap on all of the creatures in this book, but the proggy technique will work with almost any fabric. Fleece is soft and does not fray; it makes a minimal amount of mess while the strips are being cut; and is lightweight, hypoallergenic, and machine washable, which makes it easier to keep the creatures clean.

Felt

Felt is a great alternative to fleece, as it creates a firmer texture but looks the same when it covers the burlap. It usually requires the same amount of material as fleece.

Cotton and T-shirt Fabrics

Strips of a woven cotton fabric will fray, so make the strips longer than recommended—2½ x ¾ in. (6 x 2cm) is ideal. You will also need to insert the strips into the burlap so that they are closer together—two to three strands of burlap apart. This means you will need 50 to 100 percent more fabric than if you were using fleece, depending on the weight of the material.

Plastics

Recycled plastic shopping bags make a brilliant alternative to fleece. They are especially effective if you are making a water creature as it gives a shiny finish. You will need 50 percent more plastic than fleece.

Sheep's Fleece

Using wool from a sheep—especially if it's been washed but not spun—allows you to create some amazing effects for some of the fluffier animals. You may need to tie it onto the burlap to secure it. You are likely to need twice as much wool than fleece fabric to get a dense finish.

Eyes and Noses

A lot of the animals have plastic safety eyes and noses. If correctly inserted, these are secure, making them ideal for children's toys. If you are sure that children will not play with your proggy creatures, you can use buttons instead. Another alternative is to hook through lengths of fabric to make the eyes and nose.

Enlarging and Transferring Templates

The templates in this book need to be enlarged on a photocopier, or by using a computer scanner and printer, before you can use them.

Each template needs to be enlarged by 200 percent. The sections are printed in different colors to make them easy to follow. There's no need to cut out the paper templates for the burlap sections—just place them under the fabric and you will be able to see the outline through the spaces between the threads. Use a fabric marking pen with a broad tip to trace the design onto the fabric. This makes the template much easier to follow—especially if this is your first proggy creation—and there's no need to worry about the marks showing on your finished creature as they will be hidden by the proggy covering.

Each burlap section has two marked lines: an inner, solid line that marks the area you will fill with fabric strips, and an outer, broken line that is the shape you follow when cutting out the fabric. Once you have cut out the fabric, the border around the solid outline is folded over and secured in place with proggy strips to prevent the burlap from fraying as you work. This means there is no need to tack or sew the edges before you begin. It also gives you a stable edge to sew along when you join the sections together, which makes assembling the animals much easier.

When you trace the templates on the burlap, be sure to include any additional markings, for example the position of the eyes or wings and where different colored sections fall, such as on the penguin or the turtle shell. This will help you finish your project, as it is much harder to add in those marks once you have filled the section with proggy strips.

Trace the outline through the burlap, making sure you include the markings for the colored sections and any features.

Cut out the template shapes for the fleece sections as directed on the template.

Cut out the paper templates for the fleece elements of the animals, such as feet, ears, and tails. Pin them onto the fleece, then cut them out. The template will state how many elements are required and which color of fleece to cut them from.

For some sections, such as the body of the badger, you need to cut two shapes from the same template. The shapes need to be a mirror image of each other so you must flip the template over before marking and cutting the second shape.

Sassy Squirrel

Templates for project on pages 22–25. Shown at 50%. Photocopy at 200% to enlarge them to full size.

Tail
Gray
Cut 2 from burlap, flipping the template to make a mirror image for the second shape

Tummy
Cut 1 from white fleece

C Ear
Eye

Head gusset
Cut 1 from gray fleece

Base
Cut 1 from gray fleece

Body
Cut 2 from gray fleece, flipping the template to make a mirror image for the second shape

Ears
Cut 2 from gray fleece

Cutting line
Sewing line
Drawing line
✕ Eyes, Ears, Beak, or Joints

The template sections are shown in different colors to help differentiate them.

Measuring and Cutting the Proggy Strips

Proggy strips were traditionally measured using the side of a matchbox, which created a rectangle measuring 2 x ½ in. (5 x 1.5cm). We use a template (see right) to measure them. This size is used for all the creatures in this book except the hedgehog, which has pointed strips (see bottom template on right). Proggy is a very forgiving technique, so you don't have to be super accurate about the length and width of your strips. However, the better you are

at keeping the size uniform, the less trimming you will need to do to your finished creature. To make cutting the strips quicker and easier, you can use a rotary cutter and board and a strip snip tool.

If you want to experiment by making creatures with long, shaggy coats, or try your hand at proggy rugs, you may want to make the strips longer than this. Or you can use a variety of lengths to create raised areas to add texture to your work. Alternatively, you can try the loop technique shown on page 106.

Proggy strip ½ x 2 in. (1.5 x 5cm)

Hedgehog strip ½ x 2 in. (1.5 x 5cm)

Techniques

The proggy technique—pushing strips of fabric into burlap—is a versatile one. Making the creatures also requires some hand sewing.

The Basic Proggy Method

All the projects use the basic proggy stitch. It is incredibly simple and requires 2 x ½ in. (5cm x 1.5cm) strips of fabrics (see template on page 101). To make a stitch you must always work from the back (wrong side) of the burlap.

1 Use the proggy tool to make a hole in the burlap by inserting it between the threads to push them apart. Don't worry about making the hole too large—it will close up again when you make the next hole.

2 Use the proggy tool to push a strip of fabric about halfway through the hole, pushing it from the corner of one end rather than the center. (It is harder to push the strip if you work from the center.)

3 Use the proggy tool to make a second hole 3 or 4 strands of burlap away from the first. Don't be tempted to make the holes any closer than this or the burlap will begin to curl and you want it to stay flat.

4 Use the proggy tool to push the other end of the fabric strip through the second hole to the front of the burlap.

5 Adjust the ends of the strips as you go to keep your work even.

6 If you used fleece, or another fabric that will not fray, and your finished project has some stray strips or looks uneven, you can use a pair of scissors to trim the surface.

Securing the Edges of the Burlap

To prevent the edges of the burlap section from fraying, fold over the edges and work through both layers of fabric to secure them.

Fold the burlap along the lines marked on the template and, working around the edge, use the proggy technique to secure the edge. When you get to a curved section, "pin" sections together with pieces of fabric, then join these to secure the whole edge. This helps to prevent the burlap from bunching at one end.

Use pieces of fabric to "pin" the curved edges.

Fill in the sections between the "pins" until the entire edge is secure.

Weaving

For some animals you need to secure the edge of the burlap without using proggy strips. Do this using the weaving technique and long strips of ½ in. (1.5cm) wide fabric. To do this, always work from the back (wrong side) of the fabric.

1 Fold the edge of the burlap as marked on the template. Use the proggy tool to make a hole through both layers of fabric in the same way as for the basic proggy method (see opposite page).

2 Use the proggy tool to push one end of the strip of fabric through the hole. Pull it all the way through, from the back to the front, leaving a ¾ in. (2cm) tab at the back. Push the strip from the corner of one end rather than the center. (It is harder to push the strip if you work from the center.)

3 Use the proggy tool to make a second hole 6 to 8 strands of burlap away from the first. As you become more experienced with the technique, you can place them closer together if you wish.

4 Use the proggy tool to push the other end of the fabric strip through the burlap, from the front to the back, and pull it all the way through to create a stitch. Don't pull too tightly or the fabric will bunch up.

5 Repeat steps 1 through 4, weaving the fabric in and out of the burlap to create a running stitch around the edge.

The weaving technique creates a running stitch around the folded edge of the burlap.

Loop Stitch

As an alternative to the basic proggy method, you can use a loop stitch to make a curly coat for your animals. You will need long strips of fleece that are ½ in. (1.5cm) wide. This stitch is worked from the back to the front of the fabric.

1 Use the proggy tool to make a hole in the burlap by inserting it between the threads to push them apart. Don't worry about making the hole too large—they will close up again when you make the next hole.

2 Use the proggy tool to push one end of the strip of fabric through the hole, from the back to the front, so that about ¾ in. (2cm) is left in the front (right side). Push the strip from the corner of one end rather than the center. (It is harder to push the strip if you work from the center.)

3 Use the proggy tool to make a second hole three to four strands of burlap away from the first. Don't be tempted to make the holes any closer than this or the burlap will begin to curl.

4 Fold over ½–¾ in. (1.5–2cm) of the fabric strip and use the proggy tool to push the folded end through the burlap to create a loop.

5 Repeat steps 3 and 4 to create a series of loops on the front (right side) of the burlap. Adjust the loops as you go to keep your work even.

6 When you get to the end of the strip of fabric, push the end through to the front of your work. It's important to keep the beginning ends of the strips at the front of your work as this prevents the loops from unraveling.

Inserting Safety Eyes and Noses

Push the shaft of the eye or nose through the burlap from the front to the back in the position marked on the template. Push on the washer until it is secure.

Tying on Limbs

For some of the animals, a long strip of fleece on the limb is used to attach the legs and other limbs. The point where these are attached to the body is usually marked on the template shapes.

1 At the point marked on the template (or the desired position), use the proggy tool to make a hole in the limb by inserting it between the burlap threads to push them apart. Push both ends of the long strip of fabric through the limb from the front through to the back keeping them three strands of burlap apart. Push the strips through the body in the same way, from the front to the back.

2 Use a double knot to tie together the ends of the strip of fabric. If the creature is going to be given to a child as a toy, secure the knot with a dab of fabric glue.

Tying on Feet and Ears

Many of the creatures have feet and ears that are attached to the body using tabs cut into the fleece.

1 At the point marked on the template (or the desired position), use the proggy tool to make a hole by inserting it between the burlap threads to push them apart. Push one tab through the burlap from the front to the back. Repeat with a second tab three strands of burlap away from the first.

2 Use a double knot to tie the tabs together. If the creature is going to be given to a child as a toy, secure the knot with a dab of fabric glue.

Sewing

Assembling most of the projects in this book requires a small amount of hand sewing, but you only need four simple stitches.

Oversewing

This stitch is used to join the burlap sections together. Align the sections to be joined (with the wrong sides together) and make a few small stitches in the edge of one of them to secure the thread. Insert the needle through the edge of both sections from one side to the other and pull the thread firmly through so the stitch holds the edges together. Repeat, making the stitches ⅛–¼ in. (3–6mm) apart. Don't worry if you can see the stitches—they will be hidden by the proggy strips.

Backstitch

Some of the creatures have features that are sewn together, such as the flippers on the turtle and the puppy's tail. Hold the sections of fabric together, as directed in the instructions. Insert the needle from the front to the back of both pieces to make a stitch, then bring the needle back to the front to make a second stitch. Insert the needle into the second hole of the first stitch and back up to the front again about ¼ in. (5mm) further on to make a continuous line of stitching. Continue until the seam is finished.

Stab and Running Stitches

This small stitch is used to join two different colors of fabric, for example the ears on the bunny and the nose on the fox. Align the fabric pieces as directed in the instructions and pin them together. Working with the front side facing you, sew them together using a running stitch, which has small stitches on the right side and larger ones on the wrong side (where they will not be seen).

Proggy Possibilities

The instructions for each of the creatures include a suggestion for something you can do to make your project a little different.

The alternative ideas include scaling templates up to make a bigger animal, as well as suggested uses for the finished items, such as hot water bottle cover, doorstop, or tea cozy. The alternative adaptations for the projects often suggest different materials you can use to give your project a different texture.

The proggy technique can also be used to make fantastic home décor projects, such as pillows, rugs, and afghans. Pillows and rugs make ideal keepsakes when created using strips of fabric made from favorite clothes you and your family members no longer wear.

Pillows are one the easiest things to try, as they are simple squares, although you can try more interesting shapes if you wish. You can make a proggy front for a pillow and sew on a fabric backing.

The proggy technique was traditionally used to make rugs, and these still make great statement pieces. Working on a rug or afghan is a great way to get friends and family involved by asking each of them to add a few pieces to the design.

If you're making a large piece and want to incorporate a pattern or some writing in the design, draw a mirror image of it onto the back of the burlap so it appears correctly on the front.

If you want to have some fun, you can start to experiment with different materials, as almost any fabric, wool, or ribbon will work. The proggy technique is a great way to recycle old clothes or use up scraps from other projects. Just bear in mind that the materials you use to construct your animal will affect the way you clean it, but if your project will be decorative, then go wild!

Resources

US

Pat Catan's
www.patcatans.com

Amazon
www.amazon.com

Etsy
www.etsy.com

Jo-Ann Stores Inc
www.joann.com

UK

Craft Yourself Silly
www.craftyourselfsilly.com

Hobbycraft
www.hobbycraft.co.uk

Hochanda TV
www.hochanda.com

Amazon
www.amazon.co.uk

Etsy
www.etsy.com

and independent retailers

Friendly Fox

Templates for project on pages 10–13. Shown at 50%. Photocopy at 200% to enlarge them to full size.

Tail
Cut 2 from burlap

White

Orange

Ears
Cut 2 from orange fleece

Feet
Cut 1 from black fleece

Orange

Ear   Eye   Eye   Ear

Attach nose here

White

Front body
Orange
Cut 1 from burlap

Cut 1 from white fleece

Snout
Add orange fleece here

Top of snout
Cut 1 from orange fleece

Back body
Orange
Cut 1 from burlap

Big Bold Badger

Templates for project on
pages 14–17. Shown at 50%.
Photocopy at 200% to
enlarge them to full size.

Snout
Cut 1 from white
fleece

Tummy
Cut 1 from white
fleece

B

A

Snout
stripes
Cut 2
from black
fleece

Body
Gray Cut 2
from burlap, flipping
the template to
make a mirror
image for the
second shape

Ears
Cut 2 from
white fleece

Cutting line

Sewing line

Drawing line

✕ Eyes, Ears,
    Beak, or Joints

Eyes Cut 2 from
white fleece

Nose Cut 1 from
gray fleece

Happy Hedgehog

Templates for project on pages 18–21. Shown at 50%. Photocopy at 200% to enlarge them to full size.

Eye Eye

B

A A

Face
Cut 1 from beige fleece

Base
Cut 1 from burlap

Eye Eye

Body
Brown
Cut 1
from burlap

Body
Brown
Cut 1
from burlap

Sassy Squirrel

Templates for project on pages 22–25. Shown at 50%. Photocopy at 200% to enlarge them to full size.

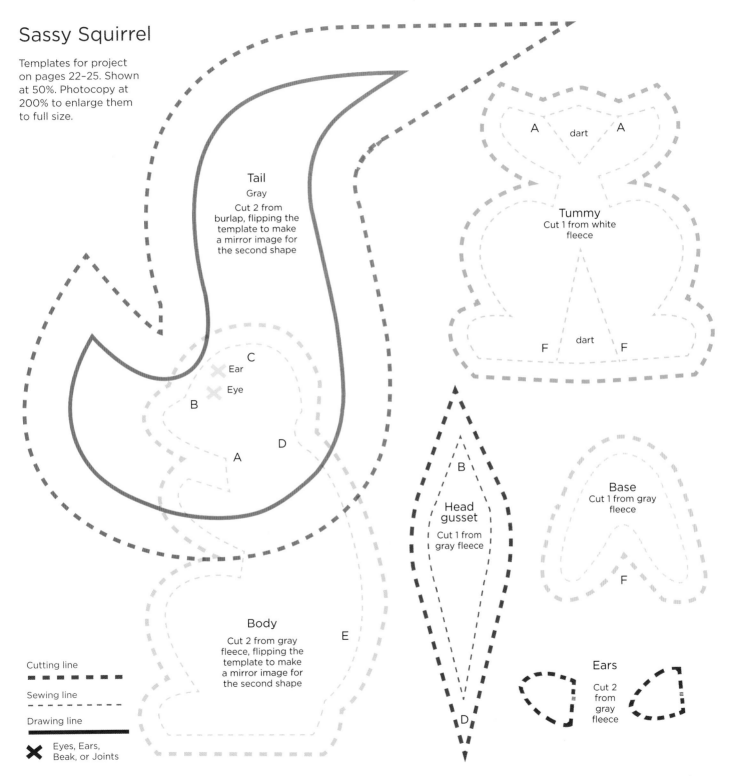

Tail
Gray
Cut 2 from burlap, flipping the template to make a mirror image for the second shape

A   dart   A

Tummy
Cut 1 from white fleece

F   dart   F

C
Ear
Eye
B
D
A

Head gusset
Cut 1 from gray fleece
B
D

Base
Cut 1 from gray fleece
F

Body
Cut 2 from gray fleece, flipping the template to make a mirror image for the second shape
E

Ears
Cut 2 from gray fleece

Cutting line

Sewing line

Drawing line

Eyes, Ears, Beak, or Joints

Little Lamb

Templates for project on pages 28–31. Shown at 50%. Photocopy at 200% to enlarge them to full size.

Body
White
Cut 2 from burlap

Add leg here

Add leg here

D

E

Top of head
Cut 1 from black fleece

B

B

A

Legs
Cut 4 from black fleece

E

Eye

Eye

D

D

C

Sides of head
Cut 1 from black fleece

Eyes
Cut 2 from brown fleece

Cutting line

Sewing line

Drawing line

Eyes, Ears, Beak, or Joints

Pink Pig

Templates for project on pages 32–35. Shown at 50%. Photocopy at 200% to enlarge them to full size.

Nose
Cut 1 from dark pink fleece

Body
Pink
Cut 2 from burlap, flipping the template to make a mirror image for the second shape

Eye

A

B

C

D

Base
Pink
Cut 1 from burlap

C

B

Tail
Cut 1 from pink fleece

E

F F

Ears
Cut 2 from pink fleece

Spooky Bat

Templates for
project on pages
36–39. Shown at 50%.
Photocopy at 200%
to enlarge them to full
size.

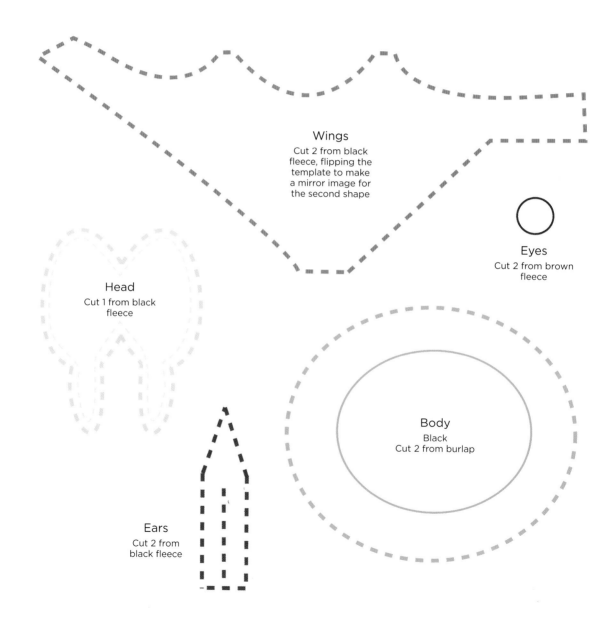

Wings
Cut 2 from black
fleece, flipping the
template to make
a mirror image for
the second shape

Eyes
Cut 2 from brown
fleece

Head
Cut 1 from black
fleece

Body
Black
Cut 2 from burlap

Ears
Cut 2 from
black fleece

Fluffy Duck

Templates for project on pages 40–43. Shown at 50%. Photocopy at 200% to enlarge them to full size.

C

Eye

Add bill here

Body
Yellow

B

Attach wing to body here

Cut 2 from burlap, flipping the template to make a mirror image for the second shape

A

Wing
Yellow

Attach wing to body here

Cut 2 from burlap

B

Tummy
Yellow

Cut 1 from burlap

Attach feet here

A

Feet
Cut 1 from orange fleece

E

Bill
Cut 2 from orange fleece

F

Cutting line

Sewing line

Drawing line

✘ Eyes, Ears, Beak, or Joints

Cuddly Kitten

Templates for project on
pages 46–49. Shown at
50%. Photocopy at 200% to
enlarge them to full size.

Ears
Cut 2 from
black fleece

Nose
Cut 1 from pink
fleece

Attach
foot to leg

Feet
White
Cut 2 from
burlap, flipping
the template to
make a mirror
image for the
second shape

G

White

Eye

F

Tail
Black
Cut 1
from
burlap

A   A

B

F

Side
Black

Cut 2 from burlap,
flipping the
template to make
a mirror image for
the second shape

D

D

C

Attach
foot

A

A

H   E

Front
White
Cut 1 from burlap

E

E   E

Darling Puppy

Templates for project on pages 50–53. Shown at 50%. Photocopy at 200% to enlarge them to full size.

Body
Beige
Cut 2 from burlap, flipping the template to make a mirror image for the second shape

A — Nose
Ear
Eye
B
C
D
E

Base
Beige
Cut 1 from burlap
C
D

Right Ear
Cut 1 from beige fleece

Left Ear
Cut 1 from beige fleece

Chin
Beige
Cut 1 from burlap

Tail
Cut 1 from beige fleece
F
Fold
G

Cutting line
Sewing line
Drawing line
✕ Eyes, Ears, Beak, or Joints

Floppy Bunny

Templates for project on pages 54–57. Shown at 50%. Photocopy at 200% to enlarge them to full size.

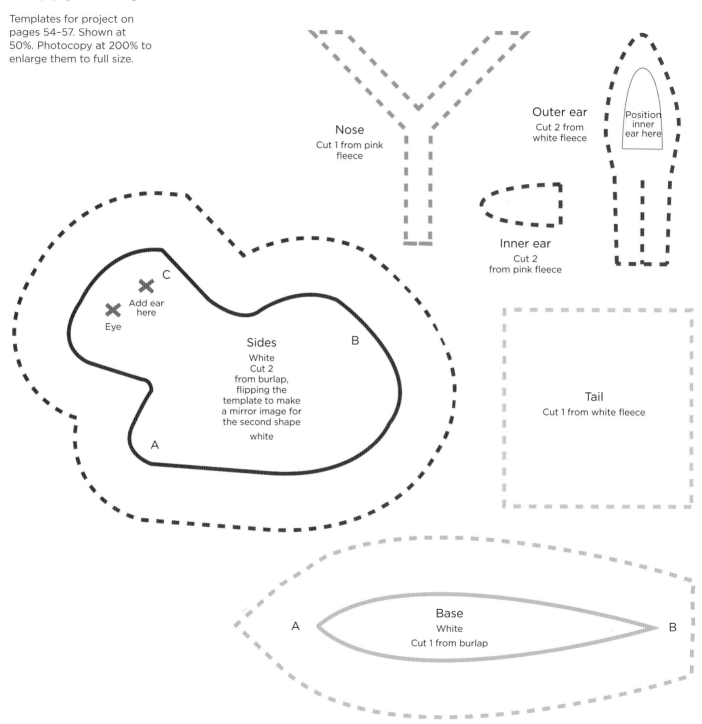

Nose
Cut 1 from pink fleece

Outer ear
Cut 2 from white fleece

Position inner ear here

Inner ear
Cut 2 from pink fleece

C

Add ear here

Eye

Sides
White
Cut 2 from burlap, flipping the template to make a mirror image for the second shape
white

B

A

Tail
Cut 1 from white fleece

A

Base
White
Cut 1 from burlap

B

Tiny Tortoise

Templates for
project on pages
58–61. Shown at 50%.
Photocopy at 200%
to enlarge them to
full size.

Legs
Cut 4 from
dark green
fleece

Shell base
Cut 1 from
burlap

Shell
Dark and bright
green fleece
Cut 1 from burlap

Head
Cut 1 from dark
green fleece

Head
Cut 1 from dark
green fleece

Cutting line

Sewing line

Drawing line

✗ Eyes, Ears,
Beak, or Joints

Pretty Parrot

Templates for project on pages 64–67. Shown at 50%. Photocopy at 200% to enlarge them to full size.

Wing
Blue
Cut 2 from burlap

Join wing to body here

Eye

Sew white face section here

Join wing to body here

Yellow

Body
Blue
Cut 2 from burlap, flipping the template to make a mirror image for the second shape

B
Beak top 1
E   A

Cut these pieces from white fleece

B
Beak top 2
C   F

Tack together here

Tail 1
Cut 1 from yellow fleece

B
Beak center
A   C
D

E
A
D
Beak base 1

Cut these pieces from black fleece

C   F
D
Beak base 2

Tail 3
Cut 1 from blue fleece

Eye
Face
Cut 1 from white

Eye
Face
Cut 1 from white

Tail 2
Cut 1 from blue fleece

Wise Old Owl

Templates for project on pages 68–71. Shown at 50%. Photocopy at 200% to enlarge them to full size.

Base
Cut 1 from burlap

Outer Eye
Cut 2 from yellow fleece

Beak & Ears
Cut 2 from leopard print fleece for the ears

Cut 1 from yellow fleece for the beak

Inner Eye
Cut 2 from white fleece

Wing 1
Leopard print
Cut 1 from burlap

Wing 2
Leopard print
Cut 1 from burlap

Ear

Front
Leopard print
Cut 1 from burlap

Ear

Eye

Eye

Beak

Tummy
Beige

Back
Leopard print
Cut 1 from burlap

Cutting line

Sewing line

Drawing line

Eyes, Ears, Beak, or Joints

Rockin' Robin

Templates for project on pages 72–75. Shown at 50%. Photocopy at 200% to enlarge them to full size.

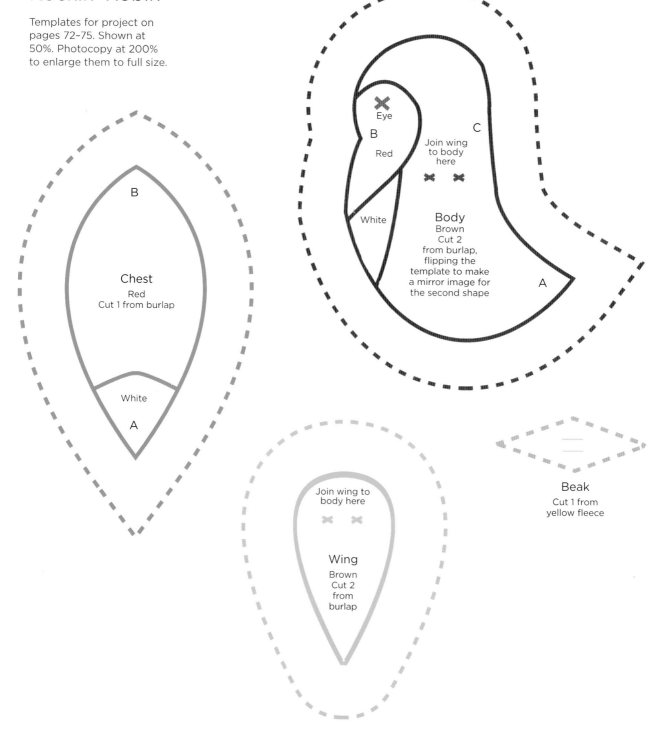

B

Chest
Red
Cut 1 from burlap

White

A

Eye

B
Red

C

Join wing to body here

White

Body
Brown
Cut 2
from burlap,
flipping the
template to make
a mirror image for
the second shape

A

Beak
Cut 1 from
yellow fleece

Join wing to body here

Wing
Brown
Cut 2
from
burlap

Baby Penguin

Templates for project on pages 76–79. Shown at 50%. Photocopy at 200% to enlarge them to full size.

Wing
Gray
Cut 1 from burlap

Join wing to body here

Black

Eye   Eye

Beak
White

Front
Gray
Cut 1 from burlap

Black

Back
Gray
Cut 1 from burlap

Base
Cut 1 from burlap

Beak
Cut 1 from black fleece

Feet
Cut 1 from black fleece

Cutting line

Sewing line

Drawing line

Eyes, Ears, Beak, or Joints

Cute Clown Fish

Templates for project on pages 82–85. Shown at 50%. Photocopy at 200% to enlarge them to full size.

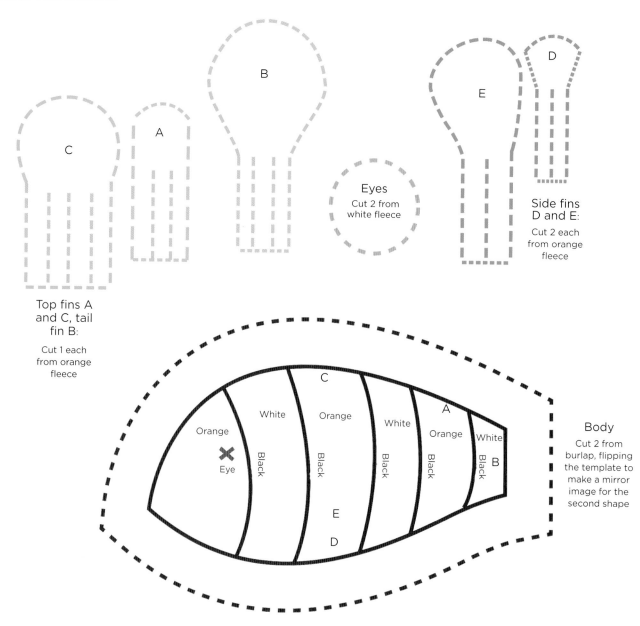

C

A

B

Eyes
Cut 2 from white fleece

E

D

Side fins D and E:
Cut 2 each from orange fleece

Top fins A and C, tail fin B:

Cut 1 each from orange fleece

Orange

White

Orange

White

A

Orange

White

Eye

Black

Black

Black

Black

Black

C

E

D

B

Body

Cut 2 from burlap, flipping the template to make a mirror image for the second shape

Snuggly Seal

Templates for project on pages 86–89. Shown at 50%. Photocopy at 200% to enlarge them to full size.

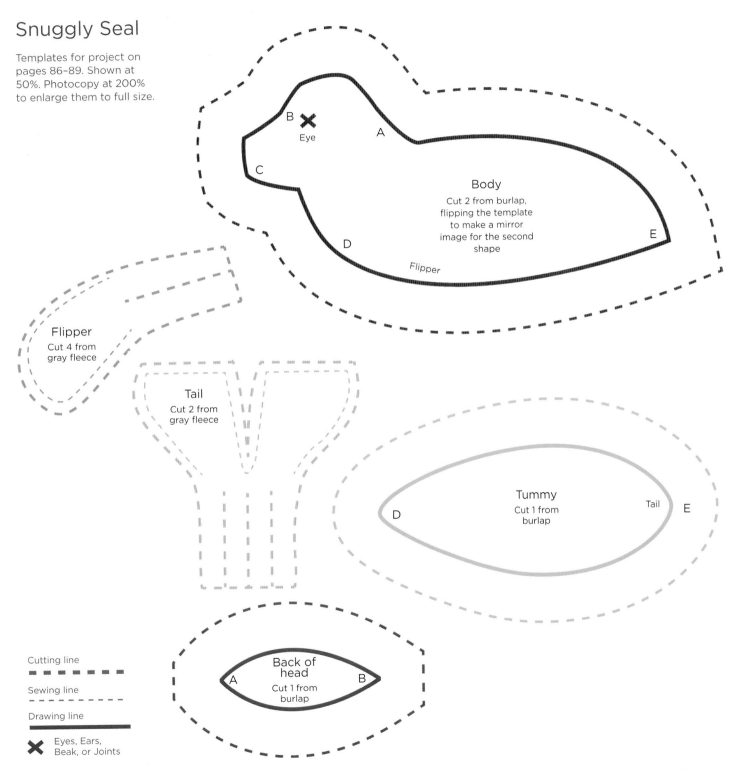

B **✕**
Eye

A

C

D

Flipper

Body
Cut 2 from burlap, flipping the template to make a mirror image for the second shape

E

Flipper
Cut 4 from gray fleece

Tail
Cut 2 from gray fleece

D

Tummy
Cut 1 from burlap

Tail

E

A

Back of head
Cut 1 from burlap

B

Cutting line

Sewing line

Drawing line

✕ Eyes, Ears, Beak, or Joints

Flappy Turtle

Templates for project on pages 90–93. Shown at 50%. Photocopy at 200% to enlarge them to full size.

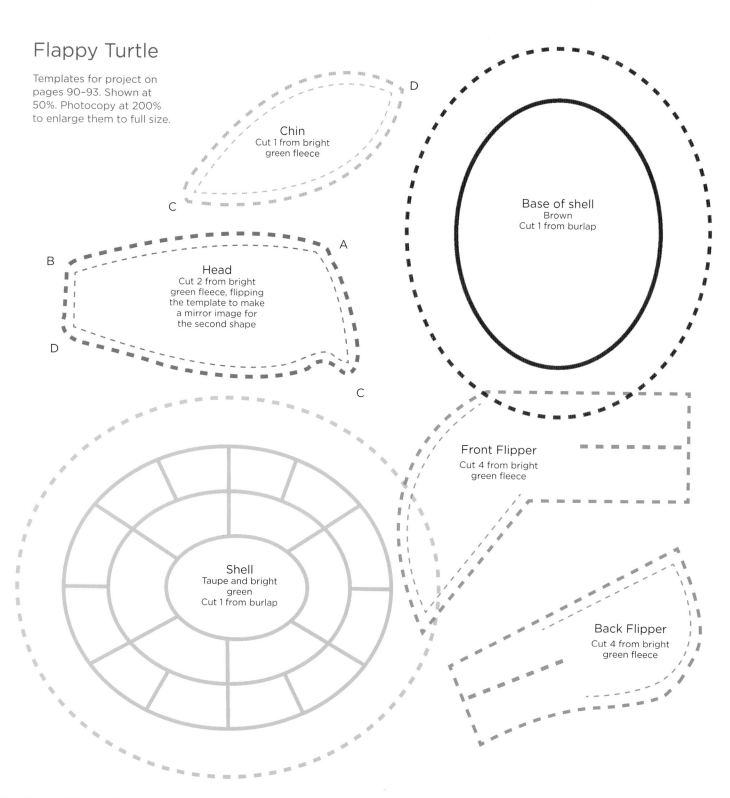

D

Chin
Cut 1 from bright green fleece

C

Base of shell
Brown
Cut 1 from burlap

B

A

Head
Cut 2 from bright green fleece, flipping the template to make a mirror image for the second shape

D

C

Front Flipper
Cut 4 from bright green fleece

Shell
Taupe and bright green
Cut 1 from burlap

Back Flipper
Cut 4 from bright green fleece

Crazy Frog

Templates for project on pages 94–97. Shown at 50%. Photocopy at 200% to enlarge them to full size.

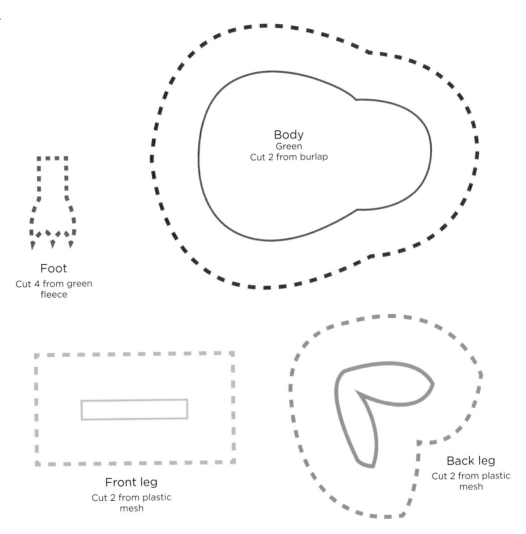

Foot
Cut 4 from green fleece

Body
Green
Cut 2 from burlap

Front leg
Cut 2 from plastic mesh

Back leg
Cut 2 from plastic mesh

Cutting line

Sewing line

Drawing line

✖ Eyes, Ears, Beak, or Joints

Index

Acknowledgments

This book is dedicated to my Nan (grandma) and Auntie Sue, who started me on my crafty journey and taught me to sew. I would also like to thank Sarah, my publisher, for taking a chance on me, and Julie, my editor, who I know had a frustrating time trying to catch me around an increasingly hectic schedule.